PIZZA CULTURA

Library and Archives Canada Cataloguing in Publication

Cirillo, Mark, 1969-, author
   Pizza cultura / Mark Cirillo.

ISBN 978-1-77126-168-5 (softcover)

   1. Pizza. 2. Pizza--History. 3. Pizza industry. I. Title.

TX770.P58C57 2017   641.82'48   C2017-906383-9

Mansfield Press Inc.
25 Mansfield Avenue, Toronto, Ontario, Canada M6J 2A9
Publisher: Denis De Klerck
www.mansfieldpress.net

PIZZA CULTURA

MARK CIRILLO

ICCO / **Mansfield** Press

Toronto / Milan / 2017

Table of Contents

Letter from the Executive Director Corrado Paina

This is the sixth publication sponsored by the Italian Chamber of Commerce of Ontario (ICCO). The goal of our organization is a very simple yet complex one: to shorten the distance between Canada and Italy, enhancing the flow and the exchange of goods, of capital, and of culture. Today the ICCO has taken a role in entrenching relationships between Canada and a Europe that has had Italy as one of its founders, and one of its most committed and sincere ambassadors in the world.

The ICCO is also the business voice of the Canadian community of Italian origin. We like to think that the Italian community in Canada has transmitted a culture that expresses itself in many ways—through architecture, design, engineering, environment, literature, art and food.

Pizza Cultura is about how Italy and Italian people were able to mix the teachings of other countries and the products from other countries to create the most eaten dish in the world.

Perhaps pizza encompasses what has always been a true element of Italian culture: the fusion of many cultures. From a small peninsula came an incredible experiment in cultural cohesion that gave birth to the Renaissance. And from a splendid city, laying in front of the sea and flanked by a volcano, came pizza. And isn't pizza similar to a 'lavic' crust with little geysers and craters?

The ICCO has called a fantastic writer and an established publisher to make *Pizza Cultura* a unique publication. This is the ICCO commitment: to perpetuate the values of gastronomy and to celebrate the fusion of cultures.

The pizza margherita—a perfect dish in its simplicity—has reached perfection through a long voyage that touched Africa, North and South America and Europe. At the end of this trip, everybody has contributed—all lands have been walked and all seas have been sailed.

I want to thank the sponsors and the contributors that made this book possible. *Pizza Cultura* is an invitation to a voyage for those who taste pizza and for a moment, let the dream take over reality.

Corrado Paina

Executive Director ICCO
Italian Chamber of Commerce of Ontario

We are delighted to present *Pizza Cultura,* a fascinating book about the history and art of one of the most beloved dishes in the world—pizza.

Pizza is indeed a genuine dish, enjoyed worldwide more and more every day. It is possibly its extreme simplicity and goodness that make it so special. Flour and tomatoes are the only ingredients you need. The simpler the recipe, the more the quality of the ingredients matters. What would pizza be without good tomatoes? A timeless duo: nothing beats the delicious flavour of authentic pizza and that's where Mutti whole peeled tomatoes shine the most! Today, pizza has become trendy, and creating a gourmet pizza with Italian ingredients has made pizzaioli become sexy from Italy to Australia, to the USA and Canada.

How do you make a premium pizza? According to the Italian traditional recipe, you need plum tomatoes, a long variety cultivated in the Southern Italian soil. Drenched with the Mediterranean sun, harvested at the peak of ripeness, and pro-

cessed the same day at a low temperature. They grant an incomparable fresh and intense flavour that cannot be reproduced elsewhere in the world. This is why the AVPN (Associazione Verace Pizza Napoletana) has certified Mutti whole peeled tomatoes: in respect of the Italian culture and tradition, they are indeed made with the highest quality standards that Mutti has always provided and you can recognize at every taste.

Both of these products, pizza and tomatoes, have changed our gastronomic culture since the 19th century. Since 1899, at Mutti, we truly and deeply love tomatoes: pursuing high quality, a fresh and superior taste—the same one you like to find on your pizza. Our mission is to bring tomatoes to their highest level, with the awareness that only great fruits can enhance your pizza to its highest level as well.

We hope you enjoy the book and you continue to enjoy pizza, authentic Italian pizza, as much as we do.

le 5 Stagioni

PIZZAS FROM THE POINT OF VIEW OF THE FLOUR

From Naples to Milan, New York to Sydney, pizza is a food that's always managed to preserve its own identity, adapting to the specific tastes of each place. It has become a global dish, embracing food culture from around the world at the same time as keeping its essence intact.

It's simple yet never dull: just a few, easily identifiable, basic ingredients strike the right balance in a pizza, creating incredibly satisfying results.

It's healthy and nutritious food: cereals as a base with tomato and dairy products on top, plus a drizzle of extra virgin olive oil, which are easy to digest if prepared in the right way.

It's a reasonably priced dish: however precious its ingredients may be, a pizza is always affordable for everyone.

It's easy to eat: it's elegant on the dish and, once it's been cut, you can eat it with your hands.

It's beautiful and well-balanced to look at: the pure white of the mozzarella stands out against the fiery red of the tomato and the green of the basil adds a touch of freshness and vibrancy.

It tastes good: chewing on this easy-to-eat dish releases the aromas and fragrances of its ingredients, with the sweetness of the well-risen dough supporting the delicate acidity of the tomato and mozzarella.

The dynamism of the pizza has become a symbol for our families' passion for the art of milling. In fact, through our brand "Le 5 stagioni" ("The 5 seasons"), our families, the Agugiaros and the Fignas, were the first to team up with pizza chefs from all over the world.

QUEEN
MARGHERITA
PIZZA

Something magical happens when you surround yourself with the people you love and eat great pizza. For me, this is a Sunday evening childhood memory... my Mother and Grandmother labouring over dough, fresh tomato sauce and soft mozzarella to create mouth watering pizzas for unexpected visitors, as people keep rolling in for Sunday evening visits, while my father kept the vino flowing.

Queen Margherita Pizza was born with the intention of recreating these magical moments. We have created a pizza that focuses on quality ingredients and sourcing of the very best products we could find.

As our pizzas take their rustic shape, Queen Margherita Pizza sets its sights on re-introducing families to family dinners.

The Toronto dining scene has such diverse offerings, with many industry leaders. To be considered one has been extremely satisfying. Our journey is a constant work in progress, we are constantly pushing new boundaries. Queen Margherita Pizza relies on a strong partnership with our ownership group, managers and most importantly our family of amazing and dedicated employees.

Queen Margherita Pizza continues to preserve Italian tradition and showcase our Canadian culture by celebrating the marriage of authenticity and diversity in The Queen Margherita Pizza dining experience.

A family that eats together stays together, Bon Appetit!

We at Aurora Importing & Distributing are proud to sponsor the *Pizza Cultura* book published by the Italian Chamber of Commerce of Ontario. This book is a wonderful opportunity to celebrate the pizza culture, it's history and versatility. Authentic, quality Italian ingredients are the cornerstone for great tasting recipes. For over 60 years, we have been serving the Italian community, importing only the highest quality, authentic ingredients and products for Canadian meals. Great Food has no borders.

Nuova Service follows in search of food excellence, and for the export of what is made best in Italy, we propose only the best products from the Italian tradition, carefully selecting the most particular ones.

With our work we offer the opportunity to small food artisans to make their product known outside their national territory, giving value to the work that makes Italy unique in the world.

Nocerino Salvatore
CEO—Nuova Service srl

The Flour of Naples. The strength and tradition. The Caputo 1924 baking range offers the very best in quality flour. The Mill of Naples since 1924, Caputo works wheat with generosity and passion so as to offer professionals and baking connoisseurs the very best in quality flour, produced with great respect for the raw ingredients and traditions. The experience developed over three generations of Master Neapolitan Millers means that Caputo guarantees extremely high standards of quality so that expert restaurateurs and skilled artisans can express their creativity to their full potential. The quality and value of our products is recognized and appreciated all around the world, thanks to our ability to preserve the natural authenticity of flavours. This is achieved using innovative processing techniques which still respect all the oldest traditions, which require the use of wheat alone, skillfully selected and mixed using a slow grinding process. Prestige, spontaneity and tradition.

THIS IS THE ART OF CAPUTO, THE ONLY MILL IN NAPLES.

Pizza Nova is proud to sponsor The Italian Chamber of Commerce as they celebrate the cultural impact of pizza past and present—through Pizza Cultura. We believe that the fundamentals of pizza are the dough, the sauce and the cheese—a foundation for great tasting pizza. But we know that pizza is so much more. It is a food experience that evokes the imagination of those who order it, brings people together with its inherent shareability and through this it creates a lifetime of memories for those who enjoy it. Once again, congratulations on capturing the indelible impact of pizza.

Tanti Auguri,
Domenic Primucci

Unico and Primo's relationship with the Italian Chamber of Commerce of Ontario has continued to grow over the years. Our companies' long standing tradition and our products represent the culture of Italian cuisine. We benefit tremendously from the continuous interaction and communication we receive from the ICCO as well as the outstanding events they put on throughout the year.

It is extremely important to all our companies that we maintain a connection and communicate with the Canadian Italian business community. The ICCO does a terrific job keeping everyone in touch.

MUTTI
SOLO POMODORO.
PARMA

Since 1831
le 5 Stagioni
LA PASSIONE PER LA PIZZA

Viva Napoli
PIZZERIA®

QUEEN
MARGHERITA
PIZZA

Unico
CELEBRATING · CÉLÉBRONS
1917 100 2017
years in Canada / ans au Canada

PRIMO
Tradizione e Qualità dal 1954

CAPUTO
1924
Il mulino di Napoli

PIZZA NOVA®

NS Nuova Service
Global Trading & Logistics

Aurora
ESTR/DEPUIS · 1955

Pizzeria
VIA MERCANTI

STELVIO
NORTHERN ITALIAN RESTAURANT

NODO

Longo's
a fresh tradition™

CHEESE BOUTIQUE

italiana
FOOD TECH

CENTENNIAL
COLLEGE
50
1966-2016

Numage Trading Inc.

PAESE MIO
AUTHENTIC ITALIAN

Monte Carlo Inns
'Your Home Away From Home'

IL GATTO NERO

bar
BUCA

WITH THE SUPPORT OF

ITA
ITALIAN TRADE COMMISSION
DELEGATION COMMERCIALE D'ITALIE

Preface

Why Everybody Loves Pizza
by Mark Cirillo

Around the time I started this project I ran into my friend, Chris Monette, a Toronto-based filmmaker, and told him I was writing a book about pizza. His reaction was similar to a lot of people I've talked to during the project: A book about pizza? I love pizza!

In no time, we were taking an animated trip down memory lane, reminiscing about the good ("I still love Pizza Nova, it's the sauce"), the bad ("Frank Vetere's deep dish!"), and many variations in between ("remember those take-home glasses from Mother's Pizza?").

He told me about his recent cycling tour of Italy, where pizza was the staple food of his many stops across the peninsula. And about his 10-year-old pizza aficionado son who adores "real Italian pizza" (Pizzeria Libretto is his favourite) not the "fast food stuff like Pizza Hut."

A SHORT FILM ABOUT PIZZA

At a certain point we circled back to the question: what makes this food so popular? Why does everybody love pizza? Chris was so intrigued by the questions he decided to make a little exploratory film about it.

He interviewed experts like Sam and Domenic Primucci (owners of Pizza Nova), chefs Massimo Bruno and Luciano Schipano, and business owners like Alda Morais (Pizzaiolo Gourmet Pizza). He spoke with people at the Italian Chamber of Commerce of Ontario, the agency that commissioned this book. And he talked to friends and family, lay people who simply have a passion for pizza (there was no shortage of volunteers).

Despite its popularity—or maybe because of

Wood-burning oven at Pizzeria Defina on Roncesvalles Ave. Photo: Rick O'Brien

Portrait excepts from *A Short Film About Pizza* by Chris Monette.

it?—everybody had their own ideas about why people love pizza so much. There were many different perspectives but we were able to distinguish these four recurrent themes.

1. IT MAKES YOU HAPPY

People have a strong emotional attachment to pizza because of experiences they associate with it. It's comfort food that reminds them of childhood, family get-togethers, and birthday parties. It's a social food; a treat for special occasions; an informal food you can eat with your hands. And because it's always there with you over the years it has a certain nostalgia to it, like an old friend you can sit down and reminisce with about the old days.

2. IT'S EASY

Old friends—like pizza!—are also easy to be with. You can just relax, be yourself. People talked about moving days, late nights at work, end-of-the-week evenings when the fridge is empty. About times when you're tired, and then you think about having a pizza, and suddenly everything's going to be alright. It'll come quickly, you don't have to fuss with cutlery, and you can customize your order to everyone's taste ("half pepperoni and cheese, half prosciutto with arugula… "). Pizza is a whole meal in a single dish. And as one person put it, when you order pizza, it's never going to go that bad: "it could be great, but worst case scenario, it's just alright."

3. IT'S VERSATILE

Of course some purists would never venture beyond a classic Pizza Margherita DOP, but for the other 99% there are few, if any, rules. You can get "three-for-one" slices up the street from my home in downtown Toronto for $5, or hop on a plane to New York City and order a $2,000 gold-plated pizza at Industry Kitchen. There are pizza bagels, pizza cones, pizza pops, pizza rolls and pizza pastries; cheese- and meat-stuffed pizzas; and pizzaghetti (a pizza topped with spaghetti). There's every style of pizzeria imaginable, from Halal to Chicago deep dish to Roman pizza al taglio.

One person likened pizza's diversity to Canada itself, a "melting pot" of global cultures. (Or is it a mosaic?). Others said there's a pizza for everyone's taste, or for every day of the week, or for different stages of your life (fun kid pizzas; serious adult pizzas). It seems that pizza is not one dish, but many.

4. IT'S ACCESSIBLE

Because of everything said above, and the fact that it's made from a few, simple, inexpensive ingredients, pizza is accessible to everyone, regardless of income level or cultural background. (One person said there are pizza-like products in every culture, like naan or laffa or pita. Another called it "approachable.") With a little time and know-how, it's even fun and easy to make, an activity that family and friends can enjoy together.

No matter how successful the industry gets, pizza itself remains a sentimental favourite—the people's dish, a perennial underdog—in the

eyes of many. Maybe that's why so many of us like to think of our favourite pizza as the most authentic one (*verace*, old school, the real deal). Or why Canadians (like Italians) tend to drink beer instead of wine with their pizza. (Inviting the guys over to watch the game over a pizza and some pinot grigio just doesn't work, we were told.)

WHAT IS PIZZA CULTURA?

This idea about the "accessibility" of pizza reminds us of its origins in eighteenth century Naples, where it was the daily food of the *lazzaroni*, the city's poorest inhabitants. It was typically sold and eaten on the street, without plates or cutlery, folded twice-over (al libretto) so the toppings wouldn't fall to the ground.

That was the story of pizza, it was just another traditional, regional flatbread in Italy, until a mass wave of Southern Italian emigration brought it to America at the beginning of the twentieth century. There, similar to Naples, it remained an urban, ethnic street food of American "little Italies" until after World War II.

It was the post-war economic boom in both Italy and the US that drove pizza's popularity within those countries and beyond, eventually becoming the global dish we know today. It was also during this period that pizza first arrived here in Ontario, via a New York City bakery called Vesuvio.

As its name suggests, this book is about the culture of pizza: the history, the varieties and the craft; the business of pizza, the people who make it, the ingredients they use. It's a reflection on a global movement but filtered through our city's local manifestations of it.

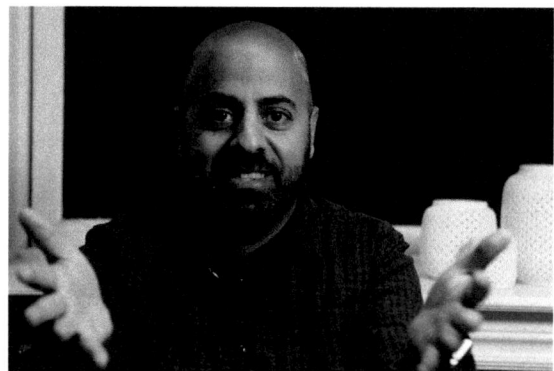

In fact, Toronto, the bustling, modern, multicultural urban centre with one of the largest Italian populations outside of Italy and its proximity to Northeastern USA, just might be the perfect place to observe pizza cultura in action.

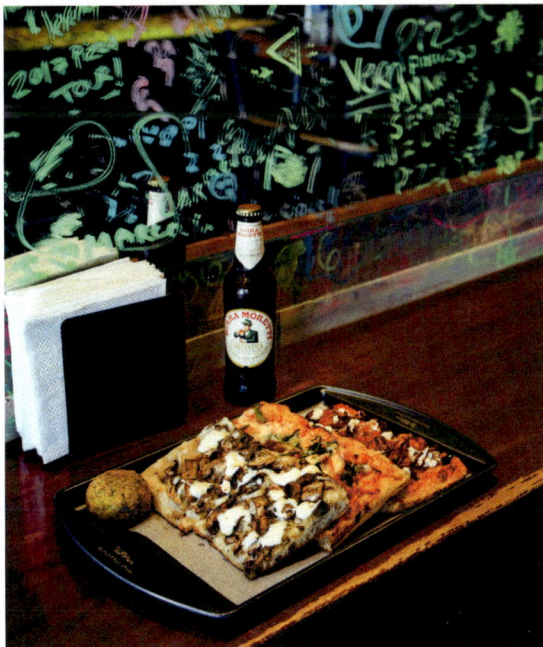

Birra Moretti at Ciao Roma, Vaughan. Photo: Rick O'Brien

Krombacher Pils at Goodfellas, Etobicoke. Photo: Werk Creativ

Italian Flatbreads

Precursors To Pizza

Flatbread is one of the world's oldest prepared foods, dating back at least 10,000 years to the early Egyptians, and a key factor in our evolution from nomadic to domesticated societies all across the globe. Already in antiquity there were many examples, made from a variety of grains, in North Africa, South Asia, Europe and Central America.

Italy, an ancient country renowned for its geographic, climatic and culinary diversity, boasts many varieties of traditional flatbreads found in each of its 20 distinct regions. In many cases their origins date back to the Romans or Etruscans, several thousand years before pizza was invented in the southern region of Campania.

Before we turn our attention to pizza—the world's most famous flatbread—here's a small sampling of the many other varieties found across the Italian peninsula.

UNLEAVENED FLATBREADS

PIADINA ROMAGNOLA

One of Italy's thinnest and best known unleavened flatbreads is a specialty from the northern region of Emilia-Romagna and dates back to the Renaissance era (14th century). Traditionally piadina was cooked on a terracotta plate (called "una teglia" in local dialect), but today it's more typically made on a metal or refractory stone stovetop pan. And while contemporary and North American adaptations often call for olive oil, true piadina romagnola is made with lard (from the Mora Romagnola breed of pig, if you want to be 100% precise).

Rolled flat before they are cooked, piadine are small in size (20-30 cms) and very malleable, perfect for folding into a *panino* (sandwich).

Left: Cecina Toscana by Gaia Massai. Photo: Rick O'Brien

21

Prosciutto crudo, stracchino cheese and arugula make up a classic piadina panino, but there are many variations, including a few sweet ones like *piadina con gianduja*.

While homemade piadina remains a very popular dish in Emilia-Romagna, it has also become a very common street food. *Chioschi di piadina* (vertically striped kiosks of various colours) are found throughout the region, on busy city streets and popular coastal areas during tourist season.

CRESCIA MARCHIGIANA OR CRESCIA URBINATE

Crescia is a type of flatbread from the central coastal region of Le Marche, and the most famous variation is called *crescia urbinate* because it hails from the walled medieval city of Urbino. In popular usage it is sometimes called *piadina sfogliata* to distinguish it from its more famous cousin from the north.

Crescia urbinate might look like piadina but it's quite different in its ingredients, taste and method of preparation. *Sfogliata* means "leafed" and refers to the many layers of dough that are folded and pressed to give the crescia dough its distinctive texture. The folding method itself is quite unique: the dough is flattened into a large sheet and rolled thin (about 3 mm), then the rolls themselves are wound into coil formations.

Piadina Romagnola. Photo: Ilaria Mazzoni

Finally, the coiled disk of double-rolled dough is flattened again before being cooked. If it's made correctly a distinctive swirl can be seen on the surface of the crescia.

Like its preparation method, the ingredients for making crescia are more elaborate than those of piadina. Eggs, lard, and whole milk give the dough a richer, creamier, fattier consistency. And the added use of fresh black pepper—historically considered a luxurious ingredient, accessible only to the aristocracy—give it an added air of no-

Above: The elaborate preparation of Crescia Marchigiana. Photo: Viviana dal Pozzo
Left: Piadina Romagnola with prosciutto, stracchino and arugula. Photo: Ilaria Mazzoni

23

Crescia Marchigiana. Photo: Viviana dal Pozzo

bility. Little wonder that the famous poet Giovanni Pascoli sang its praises, or that Duke Federico III da Montefeltro was one of its first admirers.

PIZZA SCIMA ABRUZZESE

Pizza scima means "silly pizza" —a simple dish from the south-central region of Abruzzo that evidently does not take itself too seriously. Traditionally it is cooked *al coppo*—the dough is placed directly on the hearth, and covered with a preheated cast iron or refractory-stone lid, which is then covered with embers to ensure the bread bakes evenly on both sides.

Pizza scima is an unleavened bread, likely an influence of the region's sizable Jewish population that has inhabited the area since the 17th century. In most areas along the Trabocchi coast

Above: Traditional preparation pizza scima abruzzese.
Photos: Carmelita Cianci

it is made with four simple ingredients: soft wheat flour, water, salt, and extra virgin olive oil. In some areas like the city of Lanciano white wine is added to the dough, and in others, baking soda is used to make it fluffier.

Before the dough is baked it is customary to make a rhombus-patterned incision across the top. This makes it easier to break up the pizza scima (which has crumbly texture) by hand once it's baked.

FARINATA DI CECI OR CECINA

Farinata (as it is called in Northern Italy) or cecina (as they say in Tuscany) is a thin, unleavened flatbread made of chickpea flour (*farina di ceci*) —an ingredient many people would associate with Middle Eastern or South Asian cuisine.

It was from their Tunisian rulers, during the Emirate of Sicily period (9th to 13th centuries) that Sicilians learned the art of making chickpea flour. To this day, *panella*—deep fried chickpea fritters—remain popular in the region.

The use of farina di ceci spread across the peninsula over centuries and became quite popular in the central regions of Umbria and Tuscany, an area so famous for its love of legumes its inhabitants are sometimes referred to as *mangiafagioli*, "bean eaters."

Only a centimetre in width and very pliable, cecina has an earthy, almost smokey flavour, and pairs perfectly with a glass of Chianti and some pecorino cheese—a very typical farmer's lunch.

LEAVENED FLATBREADS

TORTA AL TESTO

Torta al testo is a typical flatbread from the central region of Umbria, which is flanked by Tuscany to the west and Le Marche to the east. Like many traditional foods dating back to antiquity, it goes by various names in its native region: *torta bianca, crescia, ciaccia*. But *torta al testo* is the accepted standard outside of Umbria.

Torta means "cake" or "pie"; *un testo* is a cast iron pan on which this bread is typically cooked (the Romans used terracotta). Torta di testa is made on a stove-top rather than baked, but the dough is leavened, so it's airier and softer than piadina, yet more dense than focaccia.

Umbrian cuisine is famous for its hearty stews and torta di testo is the perfect companion, ideal for sopping up every last drop of delicious sauce. It's also very commonly used for making panini.

Cecina toscana by Gaia Massai. Photo: Rick O'Brien

Umbrian "testo" (cast iron pan). Photo: Michelle Capobianco

Focaccia Genovese

FOCACCIA

The word "focaccia" comes from the Italian "fo-colare," meaning "hearth," the floor of the fire-place—because that's where Italians baked their focaccia from Roman times right up until the middle of the 20th century, when gas and elec-

tric ovens began to proliferate during the post-war "economic miracle" period in Italy.

Today focaccia is typically baked on large, rect-angular baking sheets at medium-high heat, and cut into squares for serving. It's delicious fresh out of the oven, but most often served on platters at room temperature, accompanied by meats, cheeses, olives, and many other foods—the way Italians generally consume any type of bread.

FOCACCIA GENOVESE (OR FOCACCIA LIGURE)

Because it's so pervasive there are numerous ver-sions of focaccia, but *focaccia genovese* from the northwestern region of Liguria is easily Italy's most famous. Ligurians call it "fügassa" and they eat it morning, noon, and night—whether it's with a cappuccino, a glass of wine, or an aperitivo. The simplicity of its flavour, seasoned only with

Schiacciata con l'uva. Photo: Sandra Panaggio

salt and olive oil, is what makes it so versatile.

There's an old Genovese saying that the baker makes his dough in the morning and bakes it at night, owing to the long, multi-stage rising process. It's this slow, six-to-eight hour process that gives *focaccia genovese* its distinctive soft yet crumbly texture.

The dough is lightly pinched by hand just before baking, to create little pockets that will hold the olive oil that's lightly drizzled on the dough before baking.

SCHIACCIATA TOSCANA & SCHIACCIATA CON L'UVA

Tuscany is also famous for its focaccia—only there they call it *schiacciata* or *schiaccia*, meaning "flattened" or "squashed." Schiacciata toscana is distinctive for its crunchy exterior and soft, almost sweet interior, owing to the fact that the dough itself contains no salt. The bread is often topped with coarse salt and rosemary and drizzled with olive oil before baking.

There's a special, seasonal variation of schiacciata that's also quite famous, called *schiacciata con l'uva* (schiacciata with grapes). Sometimes referred to as "winemaker's cake," schiacciata con l'uva is made with just-picked black or red grapes and is gifted to friends and family to give thanks for the blessings of the year's harvest.

FOCACCIA BARESE

Focaccia barese is a very popular street food from the region of Puglia, especially the area around its largest city, Bari. On the surface it looks like a cross between focaccia (for its thickness) and pizza (because it's round and topped with tomatoes). Because of its dough, made with a mix of soft wheat flour, double-milled semolina, and boiled potato, focaccia has a density that is quite distinct from other types of focaccia. The toma-

Focaccia Barese by Massimo Bruno. Photo: Rick O'Brien

toes (and sometimes olives) are pressed into the top of the dough and lightly drizzled with oregano before baking.

TIGELLE OR CRESCENTINE MODENESI

Literally translated, the word *tigella* refers to a terracotta or refractory-stone disk that centuries ago was used for baking *crescentina modenese*, a small flatbread from the rural Apennine region surrounding the northern Italian city of Modena. It was common practice to carve geometric shapes into the disks—bas reliefs that would then imprint the dough itself, giving traditional crescentine modenese their distinctive, and now iconic, appearance. Today crescentine are more commonly baked in aluminum or cast iron griddles about the same size (15 cms wide, 1.5 cms high) as their terracotta predecessors.

Crescentine Modenesi. Photo: Sono Ylenia

As crescentine gained popularity beyond the "comune" of Modena they became better known as "tigelle"—a trend the locals generally resist. In fact, in 2016 the *Gazzetta di Modena* conducted a poll and found that two thirds of the city's citizens (64%) preferred *crescentini* over *tigelle*.

Crescenze are heavier than most flatbreads because they're made with whole milk and lard. The dough is leavened for several hours before being rolled and cut to size for baking in the *tigelle*. Traditionally it is served with *cunza* (sometimes called pesto modenese), a condiment made of lardo, garlic, and rosemary. But today it is just as commonly eaten with salumi, cheeses, game... even Nutella!

Finally, crescentine modenesi should not be confused with crescenta bolognese—a lesser-known flatbread from Bologna made with finely chopped prosciutto and pancetta.

SPIANATA SARDA AND PANE CARASAU

There are several famous examples of hard wheat (semolina) flatbreads from the island region of Sardinia, including *spianata sarda,* a name that literally translates to "flattened bread from Sardinia." The dough is risen for three hours before it is folded and rolled very thin

Pane Carasau

and baked at high heat—traditionally in a wood burning oven. Because of the high heat it only takes a few minutes to bake, during which the dough puffs like a balloon—similar to an Indian flatbread like naan or pekora.

An older variation of *spianata sarda*, dating back to the 2nd century BC, is the crisp *pane carasau,* sometimes called *carta musica* ("sheet-music bread") because of its parchment-like consistency. To make pane carasau is highly skilled work that traditionally requires a full day's work for three women.

The dough is rolled into wide sheets, a half a metre in width. Once they're removed from the fire's hearth they are split lengthwise and re-baked to create a *biscotto*—a dry, brittle bread that can keep up to a year.

Because of its longevity, pane carasau was the perfect bread for Sardinian shepherds, who spent months at a time in the mountains. Often, they would drizzle the biscuit with water to rehydrate it. Today pane carasau is enjoyed many ways—dry, rehydrated, lightly heated, or as the basis of many recipes, from *pane frattau* (with ragù and poached eggs) to *lasagne di pane carasau*.

SFINCIONE

The common theory is that the name *Sfinci-one* derives from the Latin "spongia," meaning "sponge," an apt description for a flatbread whose consistency is somewhere between bread and pizza.

Sfincione is a large, oval shaped flatbread that originates from Bagheria, a small coastal town just east of Palermo, where it is traditionally topped with salted sardines, onion, caciocavallo cheese, and breadcrumbs.

Today sfincione palermitana—a staple street food of Palermo that adds tomatoes to the original bargherese recipe, is the better-known version of sfincione, which has been replicated and adapted in the US and elsewhere.

Sfincione is the ancestor of the so-called Sicilian-Style Pizza which is actually an American adaptation of this traditional flatbread, often topped with melted, semi-hard mozzarella.

Sfincione

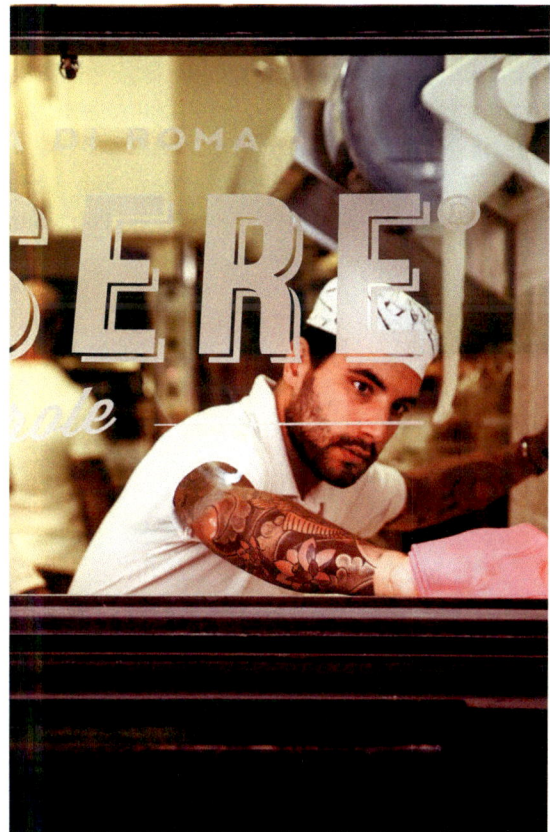

Pinsere, Via Flavia, Rome. Photo:Elvira Zilli

PINSA ROMANA

Pinsa is an ancient type of schiacciata that was common in Roman times before it disappeared for many centuries. It was rediscovered about a decade ago and has once again become popular in the Italian capital, where *pinserie* (take-out restaurants modeled on the city's famous pizza al taglio spots) have become a common sight.

"The word pinsa comes from the latin "pinsere," which means 'to stretch,' just like you do with pizza dough. In other words, pinsa is the ancestor of pizza," says Rome-based food writer Elvira Zilli.

Above: Preparation of Pinsa Romana. Photo Elvira Zilli

"In ancient times the poor that populated the Roman countryside would offer pinsa to the gods. They made it with the little that they had, using humble cereals like millet, barley and oats, plus a few herbs, water, and salt. They would give it an oval shape and bake it on flat stones over hot carbons. It was used as a plate to hold their food, like toppings placed on pizza," she says.

The modern version of pinsa is made with soy, rice, and wheat flours. It contains a high degree of water (75-80%) and is leavened for long periods of time (at least 48 hours), resulting in a flavourful and highly digestible dough.

"Similar to pizza al taglio, pinsa is often sold off the counter, already pre-shaped into rounds. The base is cooked a few minutes in the oven and toppings are added after, placed raw on top," says Zilli.

"Once you choose the kind you like from among the prepared pinsas displayed on the counter, already topped with raw ingredients, they'll bake and serve it to you hot from the oven. There are also many places in Rome where you can sit down and order a pinsa off the menu."

FOCACCIA DI RECCO (LIGURIA)

The full name of this traditional dish is *Focaccia di Recco col formaggio*, meaning a focaccia from Recco—a small coastal town in Liguria—made with cheese.

Focaccia di Recco is prepared with two sheets of ultra-thin, unleavened dough, and a layer of melted *stracchino* or *crescenza* (young, full-fat cheeses) in between. Because the dough is stretched so thin it requires a flour that is high in gluten (and therefore highly elastic) like Manitoba, so-called in Italian because it is made from a type of wheat that originates on the Canadian prairies.

Focaccia di Recco is so revered in Italy it has been granted IGP status, meaning that it is a certified and protected heritage dish.

Signage at Pinsere, Via Flavia, Rome. Photo: Elvira Zilli

Focaccia di Recco. Photo Emiko Davies

A Brief History Of Pizza

Origins In Naples
To Present Day Toronto

Compared to other Italian flatbreads discussed in Chapter 1, pizza is a relatively new invention, originating some time around the middle of the 18th century. There are conflicting theories about the origin of the term, but we know for certain that it predates the invention of pizza as we know it today. 18th century abbot Ferdinando Galiani, one of the first scholars to mention pizza (in 1789) called it a "generic name for all forms of cakes and pies," sweet or savoury, in Naples at the time. Even in modern Italian there are some dishes like *pizza di pasqua*—a popular traditional Easter cake—that have little to do with the version of pizza that has become one of the world's most popular foods.

But pizza is rarely mentioned in the literature of the era. Pellegrino Artusi's seminal *La Scienza in Cucina e L'arte di Mangiar Bene* (*Science in the Kitchen and the Art of Eating Well*, 1891), for example, makes no mention of it. This is partly because it was a regional dish associated with Naples. And more so because it was the food of the *lazzaroni*, the city's poorest inhabitants. It was an inappropriate subject for culinary literature of the time, which was written for the upper classes and aimed to document and codify the national cuisine.

THE ESSENCE OF PIZZA

If we had to distill pizza down to its essential parts they would have to be dough and tomatoes. Cheese is a third ingredient that often exists, but not always. In fact, *pizza marinara*, one of the two official pizzas recognized by the consortium for Napoletana pizza, doesn't contain cheese. And as we've seen, flatbread had been consumed with cheese for millennia, long before the relatively recent invention of pizza.

From our 21st century vantage point, it's easy to underestimate how significant it was when the lazzaroni of Naples started topping their flat-

bread with tomatoes. The association of tomatoes with pizza (and pasta) is so ubiquitous we often forget that it is not a native Italian plant and that it only appeared in Italy a few centuries ago.

DISCOVERY OF THE TOMATO

Tomatoes originated in Central and South America, and there's evidence that Aztecs and other local populations incorporated them into their diet. Italian and Spanish explorers discovered the plant in the 16th century and brought it to Europe, but they were imported for decorative purposes only.

Because tomatoes are part of the Solonaceae family (containing high levels of solanine) it was assumed they were poisonous. In certain circles tomatoes were also believed to have aphrodisiac powers—a belief reflected in the euphemistic name Italians still use for the fruit (*pomodoro*, meaning "golden apple").

The popularity and cultivation of the plant slowly grew, particularly in the area surrounding Naples, which proved to be ideally suited for the plant. And with greater supply came decreased costs. Soon the pizzaioli of Naples began using them, and by the 19th century crushed tomato was a standard topping on *pizza Napoletana*.

A final and equally critical development in the history of tomatoes in the Campania region was the rise of the canning industry. Tomatoes are perfectly suited for preserving—they retain their flavour and nutritional value for several years after canning.

Beginning with Francesco Cirio in 1867 and many others who would soon follow, the tomato canning industry grew rapidly. Suddenly tomatoes were available every day of the year and huge surpluses were being produced for export to Europe, America, Africa, and Asia. Naples' local dish became quite portable—a fact that

Riservati i diritti d'Autore a termine di legge. La presente edizione ampliata e corretta, firmata dall'Autore a tergo del frontespizio, è l'unica riconosciuta, autorizzata e completa.

→ Igiene - Economia - Buon gusto ←

La Scienza in cucina e l'Arte di mangiar bene

❀ Manuale pratico per le famiglie

compilato da **Pellegrino Artusi**

❀ 790 ricette ◆ e in Appendice "La Cucina per gli stomachi deboli" ◆ con ritratto dell'Autore

15ª EDIZIONE ◆ 58° MIGLIAIO

→ Si vende presso:

R. BEMPORAD & FIGLIO – FIRENZE, Via del Proconsolo, 7
MILANO - ROMA - NAPOLI - PISA
l'**Autore** – FIRENZE, Piazza d'Azeglio, 25 ✧ ✧ ✧ ✧
la **Tipografia Landi** – FIRENZE, Via Santa Caterina, 14 ✧ ✧

Top: La scienza in cucina e l'arte di mangiar bene by Pellegrino Artusi. Bottom: San Marzano tomatoes.

would be exploited in America by the turn of the century.

PIZZA NAPOLETANA

For the first 150 years of its existence, *pizza Napoletana* was the only style of pizza, and Naples was the only place it was eaten. It was the food of the city's poor, the lazzaroni, who would eat pizza during the week and save their pennies for a more expensive plate of *maccheroni* on weekends. Many lazzaroni lived in small dwellings without cooking facilities, so a hot meal could only be found outside of the home.

THE PIZZAIOLI

Official pizzerias were owned by *pizzaioli fissi*, "permanent" pizzaioli whose shops contained a wood-burning oven and some seating for those who wanted to eat in. There was a marble slab where the pizzaioli made his pizzas, and on prominent display in the background were the standard ingredients: fresh tomato sauce (uncooked), garlic, oregano, basil, caciovallo cheese, and cecinelli (small fish).

Because demand for pizza far exceeded the limited seating capacity of the "pizzerie," most pizza was purchased and consumed outside the shop, or taken away to be eaten at home. Many pizzaioli set up tables and sold their wares directly outside their shops alongside the city's *maccaronari* (pasta sellers). Napoletani had their own way of eating pizza on the street without plates or cutlery: *chiarselo a libretto* meant to double-fold the pizza to prevent it from dripping.

Another fixture in the streets of 19th century Naples was the *pizzaiolo ambulanto* (pizza peddler), who could be heard day or night. They would load their wooden planks with wares from the *pizzaiolo fisso*, and wander the streets and alleys of the city, singing songs and chants about how fresh and delicious they were. Citizens would open their doors and shutters and lower coin-filled baskets from upper-floor windows to get the pizza of their choice. Over time the songs of these *voci* became more elaborate, telling tales of daily life and struggles of the lazzaroni and aristocracy, and singing odes to nature and history.

PIZZA ON CREDIT

There was a third type of pizzaiolo in Naples of the time, unofficial ones who made a very different product—a *pizza fritta* (fried pizza). They were called a *pizzaiolo basso,* which means a "low" pizzaiolo, because their shops (which were really their apartments) were invariably located on the lower floor of the building in one of the city's narrow streets.

These unlicensed and technically illegal vendors offered a unique payment option to their clientele—called *pizza a ogge a otto,* which translates roughly as "pizza from today for eight days." It was a kind of pizza credit: you could eat

Sofia Loren publicity still for L'oro di Napoli.

your pizza today as long as you paid for it within eight days. And it proved popular in a city where poverty had been a long-standing problem.

The pizzaiolo *a ogge a otto* was famously depicted in the Italian film *L'oro di Napoli*, directed by Naples' most celebrated director, Vittorio de Sica, and starring its most popular female star, Sofia Loren.

THE GENTRIFICATION OF PIZZA

Despite its humble beginnings and the early perception that it was a "poor man's food," pizza would go on to become a classless, universal food.

Ferdinand IV of Naples (1751-1825) was one of the earliest known aristocratic pizza lovers who had a pizza oven built on the grounds of his summer palace. In 1880, Giovanni Brandi—owner of the legendary *Pietro e basta così* (already

more than a century old), was summoned to the court so the Savoia royal family could sample pizza Napoletana.

Nine years later (1889) his brother-in-law Rafaele Esposito was invited to the court of Umberto I on behalf of Queen Margherita (1851-1926). As the story goes, she was tired of French cuisine, which was standard at the court of the time, and wanted to try something new.

Raffaele was so excited that he showed up to the palace with his wife, Giovanna Brandi, in tow. At the palace he prepared three pizzas for the queen:

1. Olive oil, cheese and basil
2. Cecenielle (fish)
3. Tomato, mozzarella, and basil

It's also said that Raffaele ruled out making the most common pizza of the day—*pizza marinara*

Historic Pizzeria Brandi, where the the Margherita Pizza was invented.

—because it contained garlic, which was considered unfit for royal consumption.

Pietro e Basta Così has since been renamed *Pizzeria Brandi* after its famous founders, and if you visit there today you can still see a letter, dated November 11, 1889, from Queen Margherita herself, thanking Raffaele Esposito for his *buonissime* ("very delicious") pizzas.

The final and most famous anecdote of the story is that the queen enjoyed the third pizza the most, and when asked what it was called, Raffaele replied "Margherita, in honour of her majesty." Nearly a century and half later the appeal of the story is stronger than ever, firmly engrained in Italian folklore. Perhaps it's the Cinderella aspect of the queen choosing the food of the poor lazzaroni over that of the aristocracy. And of course there's the additional nationalist undertone: *pizza margherita,* Italy's famous *tre colori* dish (green, white, and red, like the flag) was chosen over its more staid French counterpart.

POPULARIZATION OF PIZZA IN ITALY

Despite the popularity of pizza today and its strong association with Italy's national image in popular imagination, within Italy it remained a *piatto napoletano* (a regional dish from Naples) until the second half of the twentieth century. It was after World War Two—during the period known as the Italian Economic Miracle (1950-1970)—that pizza culture spread across the peninsula, driven by a number of social factors.

One factor was the large-scale internal migration of southern Italians moving north in search of jobs and prosperity. They brought demand for pizza Napoletana and the skills to make it with them, and soon pizzerias started appearing across northern and central Italy.

Large numbers of Southern Italians also mi-

grated across Europe, North and South America, and Australia during this period. Everywhere they went they brought pizza culture—and as it gained popularity abroad it became entwined with the international perception of Italian culture. Suddenly tourists were visiting Rome, Venice, and Florence and asking for pizza—a dish that was unseen in those cities until very recently.

The final and most important factor was the evolution of the Italian lifestyle itself. During the Economic Miracle period the population became more urban, educated and affluent. With less time to cook and more money to spend, Italians began to eat quicker meals, especially during the week. They ate out more often. They became more experimental, trying foods beyond the traditional, regional cuisine of their parents and grandparents. And they began spending more money on "snack foods" like pizza, panini and antipasti—dishes that were ideally suited for social or cultural events or enjoyed with an after-work cocktail.

REGIONAL VARIATIONS IN ITALY

In Italy as well as abroad, pizza didn't just spread—it evolved and morphed. Some of the pizzaioli who emigrated across Italy during the post-war period set up traditional Naples-style pizzerias. But others created hybrid versions, fusing traditional pizza with local styles of flatbread.

Pizza Romana (Roman pizza) is the most famous example of this. Well before World War Two *pizza bianca* (white pizza, a flatbread without tomato, similar to focaccia) was a popular Roman specialty made in *forni* (bakeries) all over the city. It was made in large rectangular baking pans and cut into square pieces, which were sold by weight (a practice called *al taglio,* meaning "cut" or "sliced" pizza).

After the war, as pizza gained popularity all

over Italy, bakers started adding tomato as an optional topping to their *pizza bianca*, and casual establishments specializing in *pizza al taglio* began springing up across the city. Today Roman-style pizza—popularly known as *scrocchiarella* because of its characteristic crunchiness—is world famous in its own right, and *pizzerie Romane* are starting to appear in major cities around the world.

PIZZA IN AMERICA

One of the surprising facts in the history of pizza is how early it appeared in America. To understand why, consider this:

- In 1870, the Italian immigrant population in the US was 25,000
- By 1910 it was over 4,000,000

The vast majority of immigrants who came to America after the Italian Civil War were from Southern Italy. They were driven from their homeland by poverty and social and political unrest, and attracted by American recruiting efforts aimed at addressing US labour shortages, especially for unskilled workers in its growing urban centres. Many of these immigrants were from the Campania region and brought their knowledge of pizza making with them. And the cramped "little Italies" where they settled in North Eastern cities like New York, Chicago and Philadelphia were perfect settings for a kind of pizza culture to evolve.

Home-style pizza was relatively simple and inexpensive to make, and unlike many traditional foods back in Italy, its basic ingredients (flour, tomatoes, and herbs) were readily available in the US at the time. Street vendors selling pizza "al taglio"—cut to size— were also common at

Italian Immigrants arrive in New York.

the time, catering in particular to large numbers of men who had come to America on their own in order to earn enough money to bring over their families. And many Italian bakeries began making their own style of pizza with leftover bread dough.

America's first licensed pizzeria was Lombardi's, opened in 1905 by Gennaro Lombardi, an Italian immigrant from Naples who arrived in the US in 1887. Lombardi invented a coal-burning oven that could reach temperatures of 850° F in order to replicate the wood-burning ovens of Naples. And since water buffalo milk (the standard for making mozzarella in Campania) was unavailable, he used cow's milk cheese (fior di latte) instead.

In subsequent decades, many more pizzerias opened in New York, New Haven, New Jersey, and beyond, based on the Lombardi's New-York-style pizzeria. These establishments catered primarily to Italian-Americans, the real consumers (and producers) of pizza in the US up until the post-World War Two period.

Danielle Oteri, Italian-American art historian and culinary tour guide in Campania and New York's Little Italy, says the ubiquity of pizza in America today hides the fact that it was a distinctly ethnic food for many decades after the first Italians emigrated to the US. "For us pizza is everywhere," she says, "we don't even think of it as Italian food anymore. But when it first came to this country it was seen as a weird thing. The first Italians who came to New York faced a lot of racism and discrimination, and pizza was a part of that. It was a strange peasant food with garlic on it, which if you read from the 1950s, might as well have been a kind of rat poison. And it was something you could eat with your

Lombardi's in New York City, America's first licensed pizzeria. Photo: Lombardi's

hands. Many people were offended by it. So now that it's seen as this fancy thing and people talk about San Marzano tomatoes and double zero flour... it's come a long way in status!"

THE STANDARDIZATION AND GROWTH OF AMERICAN PIZZA

There's a popular theory that World War Two American soldiers stationed in Southern Italy after the Allied invasion of 1943 developed a taste for pizza, and this led to the popularization of the dish when they returned home to America after the war.

No doubt this two-year presence by American troops, mostly of non-Italian background, in Southern Italy, contributed to pizza's quick postwar evolution from a marginalized ethnic food to a mainstream dish in the US. But even more critical to the rapid spread of pizza both within America and abroad was its transformation from an artisanal product to an industrial one.

Food historian Carol Helstosky has coined the term "standardized pizza" to describe a kind of pizza that was popularized after World War Two by American chains like Pizza Hut and Domino's, as well as the frozen food industry.

It's a concise way of conveying the difference between a traditional food like *pizza napoletana*, and industrialized food that was designed for scalability from the start. Superficially, the two products appear quite similar (dough, tomato sauce, cheese, herbs, toppings),—yet they are dissimilar in almost every way. [See chart A]

As Helstosky says, standardized pizza was a convenience food created by non-Italians for a non-Italian market—competing for consumer market share against TV dinners and frozen meat pies when they gained popularity in the US in the 50s and 60s.

Coal oven at Frank Pepe Pizzeria Napoletana, New Haven, Connecticut. Photo: Tom McGovern

The scalability of the product was a key factor in its success: cooked sauce, and dry, processed cheese keep longer, and have a more consistent taste than their fresh counterparts; gas ovens are much quicker and cheaper to produce than wood-burning ones.

Standardized pizza also tapped into a new mainstream, suburban American interest in

	PIZZA NAPOLETANA	STANDARDIZED PIZZA
Flour	oo	All Purpose
Dough	Made from scratch	Frozen
Tomato Sauce	Raw crushed tomatoes	Cooked, flavoured
Cheese	Fresh mozzarella di bufala or fior di latte	Grated hard cow's milk mozzarella
Size of Pizza	8-12"	16-24"
Oven	Wood burning	Gas
Baking Temperature	900° F	600-700° F
Baking Time	90 seconds	7-10 minutes

Wood oven at Pizzeria Defina

Convection ovens are ideal for large-scale production of baked goods.

"nationality" dishes—like Chinese egg noodles and Jewish bagels, which is why stereotypical Italian iconography (the Italian grandmother, pizzaiolo, or gangster for example) often appeared in marketing campaigns for standardized pizza (and still does to this day), even though the food itself bore only passing resemblance to real Italian pizza.

Regardless of what traditionalists might think of standardized pizza there's no denying its astonishing commercial success and popularity, both domestically, and later, as the big pizza chains expanded outside US borders, globally. Today standardized pizza is found in every airport, food court and fair in North America, and there are more than 15,000 Pizza Hut locations worldwide.

Corporate growth targets and mergers, large-scale marketing, the franchising business model, advancements in food processing—so many of the factors that have propelled American-style pizza across the globe are incompatible with the artisanal nature of *pizza napoletana*. Yet, as we'll see in the chapter on tools of the trade, Italy is a world leader in pizza-making technology.

Beyond the dichotomy between Italian and American pizza is the more interesting question of whether the success of standardized American pizza has created new market opportunities for authentic Italian pizza. Could the effect of globalized pizza be similar to what happened with the international success of Starbucks coffee? Disliked by many traditionalists, Starbucks nonetheless sparked interest and demand for espresso (another Italian invention) in non-traditional markets all over the world. The quick proliferation of *napoletana*, *romana* and "thin crust" pizzerias in North America over the past decade suggests something similar could be happening in the global pizza market. Exports of Italian-produced equipment (ovens, mixers) and ingredients (San Marzano tomatoes, mozzarella di bufala) continue to rise year over year.

Consider the case of Stefano Ferrara, a third-generation Neapolitan oven maker from Naples. While his father and grandfather worked their entire careers in the greater Naples area, Stefano spends most of his time abroad, making his hand-made ovens on location at pizzerias and private residences on every continent.

PIZZA IN CANADA

Like the US, Canada has a large Italian population, but the main period of immigration occurred later here, between 1950 and 1970, when more than half a million Italians immigrated to this country. And since pizza was primarily an ethnic food prior to World War Two, it's therefore not surprising that it did not arrive in Canada before the 1950s. And it took a surprising route—via the state of Pennsylvania.

Brothers Ettore and Dominic Pugliese, still in their teens, immigrated from Gioiosa Ionica (in Reggio, Calabria) to a suburb of Pittsburgh in 1956, to live with an aunt and uncle. They had relatives in the Toronto area as well, the Commisso family, who ran several Italian bakeries. On a visit to Toronto the idea of opening a pizzeria came up: there were none in the city at the time, and given the growing population of recent Italian immigrants and the popularity of pizza in America, it seemed like a good business opportunity.

The Pugliese brothers decided to go for it. Domenic went to spend a few months with other friends of the family in New York City, the Dapolitos, owners of the iconic Vesuvio Bakery on Prince Street, where he learned the art and trade of pizza-making. Then he and his brother borrowed a truck, bought two Blodgett pizza ovens and brought them to Toronto.

They decided to call their pizzeria Vesuvio's out of respect for their mentors, and opened a storefront in Toronto's Junction neighbourhood, just a few doors west of their current location at 3014 Dundas Street West. At the height of its popularity in the 1960s Vesuvio's seated 300 people and doubled as a dance hall—serving pizzas every Friday and Saturday till the early hours of the morning. At the time Vesuvio's also operated eight satellite locations across the Greater Toronto Area.

1960s TO 1980s

Given its popularity and the fact it was Toronto's first pizzeria, it's not surprising some of the city's best-known pizza businesses were spin-offs of Vesuvio's in one way or another—restaurants like Regina Pizzeria and Bitondo's in Little Italy, Milano's in Etobicoke, and the country's biggest pizza chain, Pizza Pizza. Sam Primucci (interviewed in the next chapter) says that when he opened the original Pizza Nova in 1963 it was modeled after Vesuvio's and Totò (a very similar pizzeria that opened shortly after Vesuvio's in Little Italy).

This style of pizza, which became the Toronto standard, is a little thicker and denser in consistency than Italian pizza, but thinner than standard American pizza. It's closer in style to classic New York pizza because that's what it's based on, not the style of pizza developed by American chains like Domino's and Pizza Hut, which were products of post-war, Midwestern-US.

Another kind of pizza that was very popular in the Italian community during this period and remains so to this day is bakery pizza—usually thicker and softer in texture, closer to focaccia in

Top: Vesuvio Bakery in New York City. / Original Vesuvio's Pizza, late 1950s, on Dundas St.
Middle: Pugliese brothers outside current location in the 1960s.
Bottom: Restaurant interior and Dundas St. billboard, circa 1970.

Ettore ("Eddie") Pugliese in 2017, one month after Vesuvio's 60th anniversary. Photo: Rick O'Brien

Bitondo's, a descendant of Vesuvio's. Photo: Rick O'Brien

Superpoint, a new take on classic Toronto pizza. Photo: Rick O'Brien

consistency. It's still found in many of the city's traditional bakeries like Tre Mari (Corso Italia); Rustic Bakery (North York); Riviera (Little Italy); San Remo (Etobicoke); Francesca (Scarborough); North Pole (Danforth); Commisso Brothers and Nino D'Aversa (various locations); Aida's, St. Phillips and Di Manno (Vaughan); and more.

By the 1980s the pizza industry was a crowded sector made up of independents, restaurants, and international and regional pizza chains. It was during this period that pizza slices were popularized. And following the American lead pizzerias started adding more and more toppings, additional menu items like chicken wings, and novelty pizzas like cheese-stuffed crust.

1990S: TERRONI OPENS IN TORONTO

Canada's food culture has evolved enormously in recent decades, fueled by immigration, globalization and digital media. The Italian food sector, and pizza in particular, are perfect examples of this. A watershed moment was the opening of an Italian specialty grocer called Terroni, in Toronto's Queen Street West neighbourhood, in 1992.

Founders Cosimo Mammoliti and Paolo Scoppio had spent a great deal of time in Italy and fallen in love with its food and culture, and began with the simple idea of selling good quality, authentic Italian products. Scoppio's family, who were already in the importing business, were from Puglia, so most of Terroni's products were from that region or from southern Italy in general, including orecchiette, taralli, olives, olive oil, San Marzano tomatoes, capers, anchovies, and sardines.

Terroni also incorporated their products into casual ready-made dishes like panini and pasta al forno, and when they had earned enough to do so, they invested in a pizza oven. Not surprising-

Elena Mammoliti (with marketing manager Robby Vrenozi) talks about the early days of Terroni. Photo: Rick O'Brien

Classic Italian-style pizza at Terroni, a game-changer on the Toronto food scene in the 1990s. Photo: Rick O'Brien

ly, they wanted the style of pizza to be genuine Italian, as close as possible to what you'd get in Italy.

Elena di Maria, wife of Mammoliti and co-owner of Terroni, worked at the shop in those early days. She describes the kind of pizza they wanted to recreate as "simple, accessible, very common in Italy, but hard to find here at the time. And the idea was to do it right—the right flour, yeast, tomatoes. Something *verace* [authentic] but also very casual and affordable. I think the response was good because it's something Toronto was lacking in those days."

They followed the idea to its logical conclusions—real Italian toppings, no North-Americanized substitutes, and served the way pizza is done in Italy.

"People would come in and want their pizza cut," says di Maria, "and we'd say 'no, we want to serve it the way it's done in Italy.' We'd try to explain by saying things like, 'do you want me to cut your steak when you order one?'" It wasn't just pizza Terroni wanted to import from Italy, it was *pizza cultura*.

PIZZA NAPOLETANA COMES TO CANADA

The story behind Pizzeria Libretto, Canada's first certified Neapolitan pizzeria that opened in 2008, was remarkably similar. Chef Rocco Agostino, of Calabrian origin like Cosimo Mammoliti, and his partner Max Rimaldi (of Lazio descent), caught the *pizza napoletana* bug during their frequent trips to Italy.

"It was our experience traveling to Italy and Naples in particular that really got us excited and wanting to bring that culture back to Toronto," says Agostino. "The simplicity, the pride

Rocco Agostino makes a Margherita pizza at Toronto's first certified Neapolitan pizzeria, Libretto. Photo: Rick O'Brien

they take in it. Their way of making and eating pizza. You can go into any pizzeria in Naples and get a simple Margherita pizza that's just mind-blowing."

In fact, the term *libretto,* which literally means "little book," is itself a slice of Neapolitan culture. It's taken from the expression *pizza al libretto,* which refers to the characteristic double-fold that citizens of Naples often use to eat their pizza (especially on the go).

Agostino and Rimaldi's research led them to discover the Associazione Verace Pizza Napoletana (AVPN), a consortium for the promotion and protection of authentic Neapolitan pizza that was founded in 1984. "The AVPN is an association that establishes guidelines that help you identify what you need—the oven, the ingredients, the process—to make the real product," says Agostino.

The AVPN also provides training for *pizzaioli* (pizza makers) wanting to learn the correct way for making authentic pizza napoletana. Agostino, who prefers to call himself an "enthusiast" rather than an "expert," underwent the training and is now an AVPN-certified pizzaiolo himself.

The biggest decision Agostino and Rimaldi had to make in the early days was deciding on a wood burning oven. Working with the AVPN they discovered Naples-based Stefano Ferrara, who Agostino calls "a rockstar" because of the quality of his work and how he goes about it.

"He travels all over the world—LA, Tokyo, Buenos Aires—building these ovens by hand and really takes great pride in his work. He's a third-generation oven builder and his son is now involved, which makes it a fourth-generation business."

Rob Gentile talks about visiting Italy for the fist time and discovering pizza Romana. All photos: Rick O'Brien

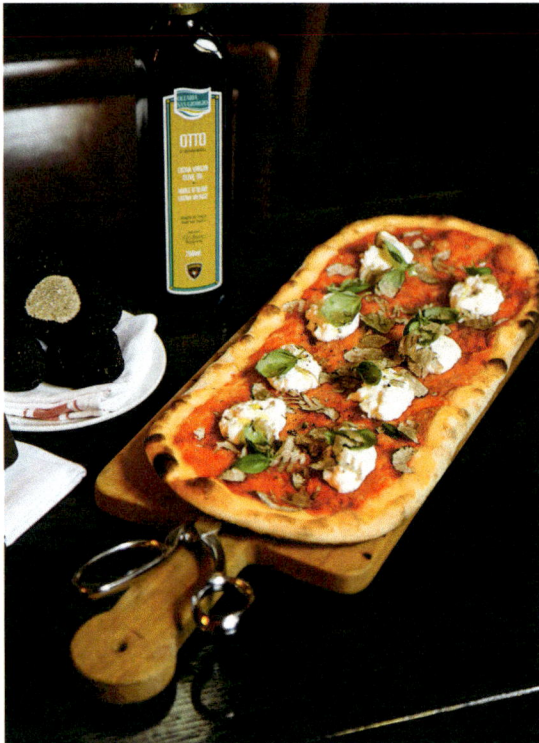

Buca pizza served on a *pala*. Photo: Rick O'Brien

Ferrara's ovens are made from the same primary materials used by his father and grandfather—tuff stone base, refractory brick dome, Biscotto di Sorrento hearth, Santa Maria brick hood, ceramic and marble exterior. "I was like a kid with a new toy that no one else had and I got to play with it," says Agostino.

Pizzeria Libretto has since opened four more locations, in addition to the Roman-style eatery Enoteca Sociale. Each pizzeria features a Stefano Ferrera oven as its centrepiece, stylishly clad in Libretto's black and white branding.

ROB GENTILE'S PIZZA MOMENT

The same year the Libretto team opened Toronto's first Neapolitan pizzeria, Buca's executive chef Rob Gentile made a trip to Italy, where he discovered a very different style of pizza.

"It was before we'd opened Buca," says Gentile, "and it was my very first time in Italy. We landed in Rome and I had the chance to explore the city, and I absolutely fell in love with Roman pizza."

Every Roman pizzeria and bakery has its own take on the Roman style. Gentile's favourites include Forno Roscioli, a family business with roots dating back to the nineteenth century, and Pizzarium, a modern take on pizza romana that has made owner Gabriele Bonci one of Italy's most famous pizza makers.

"Some places do the round pizzas. But most you see are on long rectangular trays, or they're baked directly on a stone, and it's a long oval pizza served on a *pala* [wooden paddle]," he says.

If there's one thing they all have in common it's the characteristic "crunch" of Roman pizza, what the locals call "la scrocchiarella" (a stark contrast to the malleable dough of a pizza napoletana). Gentile describes his first taste of it as a "pizza moment" that changed his perspective on pizza and became the inspiration for the pizza he developed at Buca.

"Pizza napoletana is typically made with a soft, double zero flour, low in protein, very light and airy and done in a wood-burning oven," he says.

"Whereas the Roman style pizza uses a much stronger flour—a bread flour or something high in protein. The dough is very wet, so you really need to develop the protein—you have to get a good speed on the mixer so it slaps around in the bowl. It has a long ferment, and it's usually finished in semolina. It's often served at room temperature or barely warm. For me that was a pizza moment."

When he opened Buca he experimented extensively with different flours, hydration levels, baking methods and ways of incorporating semolina into the dough before landing on the recipe that's still used today.

Vincenzo Iorio at Via Napoli.

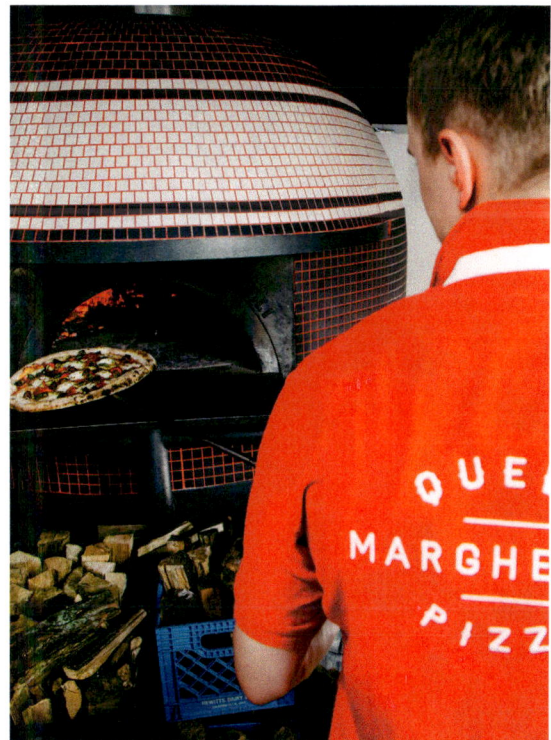

Classic wood-oven baked pizza Napoletana at Queen Margherita.

Via Mercanti founder Romolo Salvati. All photos: Rick O'Brien

Head pizzaiolo Danilo Lupo with brother team Maksym and Anton Ruzycky at Pizzeria Defina.

One of the distinct features of the Buca pizza is the way it's served on a wooden plank, uncut, with a pair of scissors. You might think the scissors are a reference to Roman pizzerias where they're often used to serve pizza al taglio, but they're actually a reference Gentile's childhood memories of eating pizza at home.

"My grandmother would always leave a pair of scissors on the table when she made pizza. That's how we ate it: you would just go up and cut yourself a piece, whatever size you wanted," he says.

"That's why I put scissors on the pizza board at Buca, rather than cutting it with a wheel in the kitchen. I wanted to serve it family style, for sharing. And you see people doing it all the time here, they cut themselves a piece and pass it down the table. It works."

THE PIZZA BOOM

Similar to many cities around the world, Toronto's pizza industry has exploded in recent years—both the business and the product. There are more varieties of pizza, and pizza makers have greater access to ingredients and toppings, than ever before.

Shortly after Libretto opened a decade ago many more pizzerie Napoletane followed suit, including Queen Margherita, Via Mercanti and Viva Napoli, to name a few. Gatto Nero, a second-generation family business from the Campania region, offers what owner Michele Raviele calls "croccante" Neapolitan pizza—a thin crust with the lightness of pizza napoletana but cooked lower and longer for a crunchier finish.

A more conventional pizza morbida can be found at Defina on Roncesvalles, the only Toronto pizzeria that offers both classic Italian styles: Napoletana and Romana (which is thinner, lighter and crunchier in texture).

Eggplant parmigiana pizza at Gatto Nero

Valerio Chiapparelli at Ciao Roma

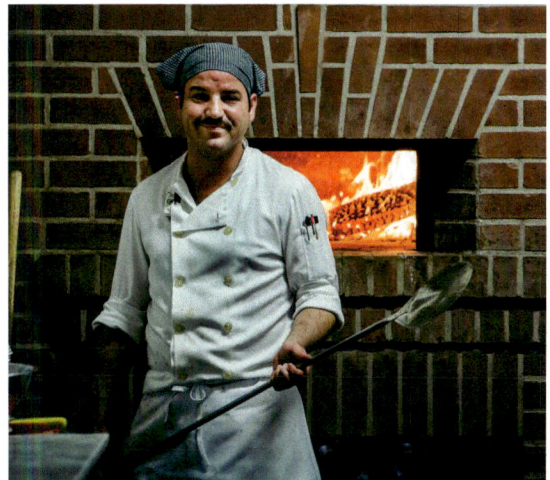
Dave Mattachioni with his wood-burning brick oven.

A few years after Buca created its Roscioli-influenced pizza, Rob Federici opened Ciao Roma, a popular Roman-style al taglio pizzeria in Vaughan. To ensure the authenticity of the product he not only went to Rome for research but brought back his mentor, Valerio Chiapparelli, to work alongside him at the pizzeria. In 2013 Cosimo Mammoliti unveiled his own version of Roman when he launched Terroni's first bakery, Sud Forno on Queen Street West.

In 2015 former Terroni chef David Mattachioni opened his eponymous bakery in the Junction, where his artisanal Italian breads and pizzas are made from natural sourdough starter and baked in a custom-built, wood-burning brick oven.

During this period, American pizza styles have also become more common around town. In 2012 Josh Spatz partnered with former Libretto chef Alex Potter and Frank Pinello (host of Vice TV's The Pizza Show) to open North of-

Top: Descendant's Chris Getchell finishes his Detroit-style pizza on the oven hearth for extra crunch.
Bottom Delivery meets gourmet at Maker Pizza. Photos: Rick O'Brien

Brooklyn, a New-York style slice shop inspired by Pinello's legendary Best Pizza.

While working at North of Brooklyn, pizza maker Chris Gretchell had the opportunity to meet Pinello, who taught him how to make pan-pizza styles like *Grandma* and *Sicilian*. After doing some research of his own, Gretchell discovered another American style, a deep-dish pizza from Detroit that historically speaking, evolved from the New York Sicilian style. When he decided to open his own Detroit-style pizzeria in Leslieville, he called it Descendant to pay homage to the pizza's venerable ancestry.

Meanwhile, former FBI Pizza owner Shlomo Buchler enlisted the services of popular chef Matty Matheson to create a playful mash-up of Italian and American, high and low culinary references for Maker Pizza, where menu items include Cool Hand Zuch, Napoli Dynamite and Dr. Pepperoni.

A little more casual, though no less playfully ironic, is Superpoint by Jonny Poon and Jesse Fader, who consciously harken back to 70s and 80s Toronto in both the style of their pizza and their choice of décor. (see page 46)

Top: Pizza al taglio at Sud Forno.
Bottom: New York Style pizza at North of Brooklyn. Photos: Rick O'Brien

A Family Pizza Chain

Pizza Nova

Sam Primucci was a teenager growing up in West Toronto in the 1950s when the city's first pizzerias started to appear. They were modeled after Italian-American pizzerias in the North-Western US, and like American pizzerias they first became popular in ethnic neighbourhoods like Toronto's Little Italy.

But it didn't take long for pizza to catch on in the Toronto region, and within a few years pizzerias were opening across the city and beyond, in places like Mississauga, Brampton, and Scarborough, where Sam and his brothers opened the first Pizza Nova in 1963.

The Primuccis were early adopters, quick to capitalize on the trend towards delivery pizza, and one of the first Canadian businesses to successfully market it in predominantly non-Italian neighbourhoods. By 1965 the Primuccis had opened their second location and haven't looked back since: today, with over 140 locations in Southern Ontario, Pizza Nova is Canada's fourth largest pizza chain.

The company has successfully carved out a niche at the high end of the pizza chain sector, marketing itself as the fresher, higher-end alternative to its competitors. Today it is run by Sam Primucci (CEO) and his son Domenic (President).[1]

IMMIGRATING TO CANADA

Sam, you immigrated to Canada in the 1950s from the town of Palazzo San Gervasio, in the province of Potenza. What's your memory of the experience?

It was in 1952, I was 12 years old when we came here. I remember it was May 1st, the Festa dei Lavoratori in Italy, the day we got on the boat. We watched the big parade along Lungomare in Napoli, it's a fantastic parade that they still do today. And then we boarded the boat. After 10 days we landed in Halifax, where we boarded a train to Toronto.

I have this one memory of being on the boat that touches me to this day. There was a young

Sam and Domenic Primucci at Pizza Nova head office in Scarborough. Photo: Rick O'Brien

57

Vesuvio's College Street circa 1960, at left, next to College Shoe Store. Photo: City of Toronto Archives

man on the boat who had a guitar, and every day he'd sing the same songs: "Terra Straniera" and "Vola Colomba."

Where did your family settle in Toronto?

Sam Primucci. Photo: Rick O'Brien

On Denison Avenue, near Bathurst and Queen. We were at number seven, just north of Queen, across from the church. We were just down the street from Italian Home Bakery: their forno was number 15 Denison if I remember correctly.

PIZZA IN THE 1950S

As a kid in Italy, before you came here, do you recall eating pizza?

Back in those days families made their own bread, but nobody owned an oven, so you would bring it to the fornaio for baking. My mother would make a batch of bread dough and whatever was leftover she would send it along with the bread.

What the bakers would do is bake everyone's bread and then at the end they'd bake all the left-

Group shot at the original Pizza Nova on Kennedy, including Sam and Vince Primucci, Pat Colangelo, Charlie Bartolotta, and Frank and Arthur Macri.

over odds and ends. They would bake them in a tray, so really it was really more like focaccia than pizza. Everyone would do their own thing, with potatoes or meat and things like that.

What about when you came to Toronto, what are your early memories of pizza?

The two places I remember going to as a teenager were Totò and Vesuvio. Not the original Vesuvio that was at Dundas and Quebec, that was a long distance for us because nobody had a car back then.

We ate at their second location, it was right beside the Pylon Theatre (now called the Royal). It was a long, narrow hallway, must have been 75 feet deep, and they'd make the pizzas right there in the window. I think it was Eddie's uncle, he was a real chubby guy.

Anyway both Totò and Vesuvio made wood-burning oven pizza. Everyone had their favourite but looking back, to be honest, they were pretty much the same thing. I'd say the pizzas were better back then because they really

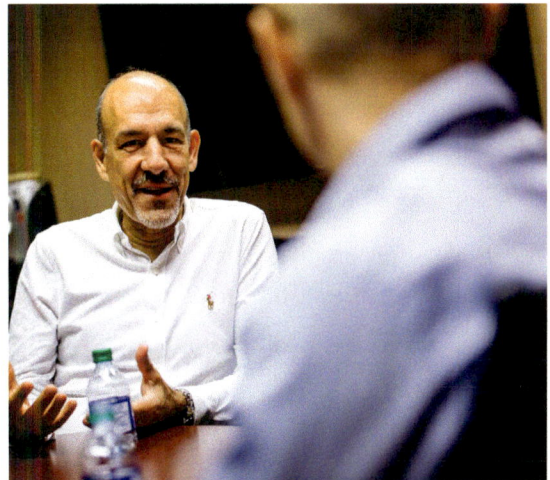

Domenic Primucci. Photo: Rick O'Brien

59

Mike, Sam, and Dominic Primucci at the Canadian National Exhibition in the 80s

cooked the pizzas—you could just pick up a slice and eat it.

Today many people complain about feeling too full after eating pizza from certain places, and I say it's because they're eating a raw product. I tell them to order it well done next time and they're always surprised what a difference that makes. You have to really cook the dough, and both Totò and Vesuvio did.

THE EARLY DAYS OF PIZZA NOVA

Tell us about the original Pizza Nova location at Lawrence and Kennedy in Scarborough.

We opened in 1963, it was mostly a delivery pizza place but we had three or four tables as well. We delivered to a wide area that included West Hill to the east and Don Mills to the west—that was a very prestigious area at the time, people like E.P. Taylor lived there.

There wasn't the traffic you have now, so we could service a wide area. Also people had different expectations: if it took an hour and a half for your pizza it was no big deal. You see, pizza was a treat back then, something you'd order on a Saturday night when you had friends over. Those were our busy nights. I mean Saturday nights are still very busy, but today pizza is a meal. Back then we opened at 4 pm; today we open at 11 am. People have pizza for lunch. They pick it up on the way home and have it with their children for supper. They take leftovers to work or school for lunch.

Who were your customers in those days—Italians, non-Italians, a combination of both?

Vesuvio and Totò served people in the Italian

The new look of Pizza Nova with its characteristic wall of canned tomatoes. Photo: Rick O'Brien

community because they were located in Little Italy. Out in the east end there were very few Italians, except on the Danforth where there were Sicilian and Pugliese communities who would order from us.

When did you start to evolve from a single pizzeria to a multi-location business?

A few years after we opened, the demand just got too high, the traffic and congestion started to go up. From Kennedy Road to Victoria Park there was only one light, on Warden Avenue, when we started. Now there's 10 or 15. So at a certain point we decided to open a second location. It was a bit scary at first!

Our second location was near Yonge and Finch, on Betty Ann Drive. Doctor Morton Shulman lived on the street, the former Chief Coroner of Ontario. I never forget! Back then you would answer the phone, make the pizza, then you'd get in your car and deliver it. You did everything. So one day I answered the phone and I had a bit of a cold. He asked me if I was sick and I said no, I'm ok. And he said, "You don't sound ok! Cancel the order!"

What did the pizzerias look like at that time? Were they anything like the ones we see today, where you can walk in and choose a slice from the pizzas behind the counter?

No, it was completely different. The kitchen was actually hidden. You had a wall, with a small wicket, and the guys would make the pizzas in the back. So the customer never saw how the pizza was made. We'd take their order down on a piece of paper and bring it back to the kitchen.

Pizza by the slice was popularized in Toronto in the 1980s. Photo: Rick O'Brien

EVOLUTION OF THE MENU

When did pizza by the slice start to appear?

It would have been in the early 80s, after we opened at Jane and Wilson. Funny thing, in the Italian community many people think that was our first location. It was very popular in the community, and all the students from the university used to come. We had line-ups seven days a week.

As time has gone on your menu has gotten a lot more complicated—from chicken wings to panini to lasagna. What are the guiding principles as you evolve?

The thing about pizza is that it's a food you eat with your hands. And it's a sharing food. That's why pizza companies started doing chicken wings, even though of course it's not an Italian

thing. Lasagna is something we've done for many years, it's a very common dish at social gatherings. We've added salads and sandwiches over the years because, as my father says, pizza has become more of a meal. So you need to have more options, for families and for single people.

We also get a lot of time orders now: people call from work at lunch time, putting in a dinner order for a set time so they can pick it up for the family. That's an example of how service has evolved—we didn't get those kinds of orders in the past.

A few years ago you added focaccia barese to the menu and went to the trouble of having it approved as an authentic traditional product by the consortium in Puglia. How and why did that come about?

[Sam] I'm not exactly from Puglia but we're pretty close—we're the last town in Basilicata before

Pizza Nova's Focaccia Barese adheres to the traditional recipe and is recognized by the consortium in Puglia. Photo: Rick O'Brien

you get there. There's one thing you should remember about focaccia barese, it's the only product that ever shut down a McDonalds. It happened in Altamura, focaccia is a staple of the region. People go to the bakery and get a slice and a drink, and they eat it at stand-up counters, like our sliced pizza.

Focaccia is a little different than pizza. You can cut it and make a sandwich out of it, use it as bread. A lot of people I know serve it with cold cuts, cheese, homemade sausage. It's more like an appetizer or snack than a meal.

When we decided to bring it over to Canada we wanted to do it right, so we worked with Consorzio in Puglia to develop our recipe. They came here and taught us the correct way to make it, so we are able to use the IGP logo of authenticity. I think they were amazed we were able to copy it to T!

For our focaccia we use Pachino-style tomatoes grown right here in Ontario, in Leamington. You don't need to salt them because they have a natural salt content of 15-20%—a lot higher than the typical 5% or so you get with other varieties.

BECOMING A PIZZA CHAIN

Pizza Nova has grown from a single- to multi-location pizzeria, from independent family business to franchisor with over 140 locations. What are some of the challenges inherent in that kind of growth?

[Domenic] The company was founded on quality. It's always been quality of the product from day one, and that's something we talk about every day at this office, and when we're on the road with our franchisees.

Domenico Caputo and his team at Pizza Nova, Rutherford and Islington location. Photo: Rick O'Brien

Over the past number of years, service has changed in Canada. Not just in this industry, in every industry. In the US it's been about service for a long time, and that mentality eventually made its way here.

It's partly about speed—people call for a pizza and they want it right away. But it's also about friendliness, personal service, which is something we try to instill into our culture. It's been a big push of ours to keep getting better on both service and quality.

It's so important to a business—wherever you go, you remember whether you've had a positive or negative experience. You're not going to go back to a place where you had bad service, even if the product is great. But if you've got great service and great product, then you've really got something.

How do you protect the quality for your products and services as you grow?

[Domenic] Simple—it's training. I say simple, but of course simple doesn't mean easy. Training is constant, it's not an event where you say we've trained you and off you go. It's something that happens every day.

Pizza itself is not a simple commercial product, you don't push a button and it's made. It's done by hand. It's a skill. So there's a lot of training that goes on to ensure we have the same product whether it's at Kennedy and Lawrence where we started, or in Mississauga or up in Huntsville.

[Sam] You and I could make a pizza with the same dough, the same sauce, the same ingredients, and they would taste completely different.

You take our toppings, we have over 30 of them today. You want to put them on the pizza

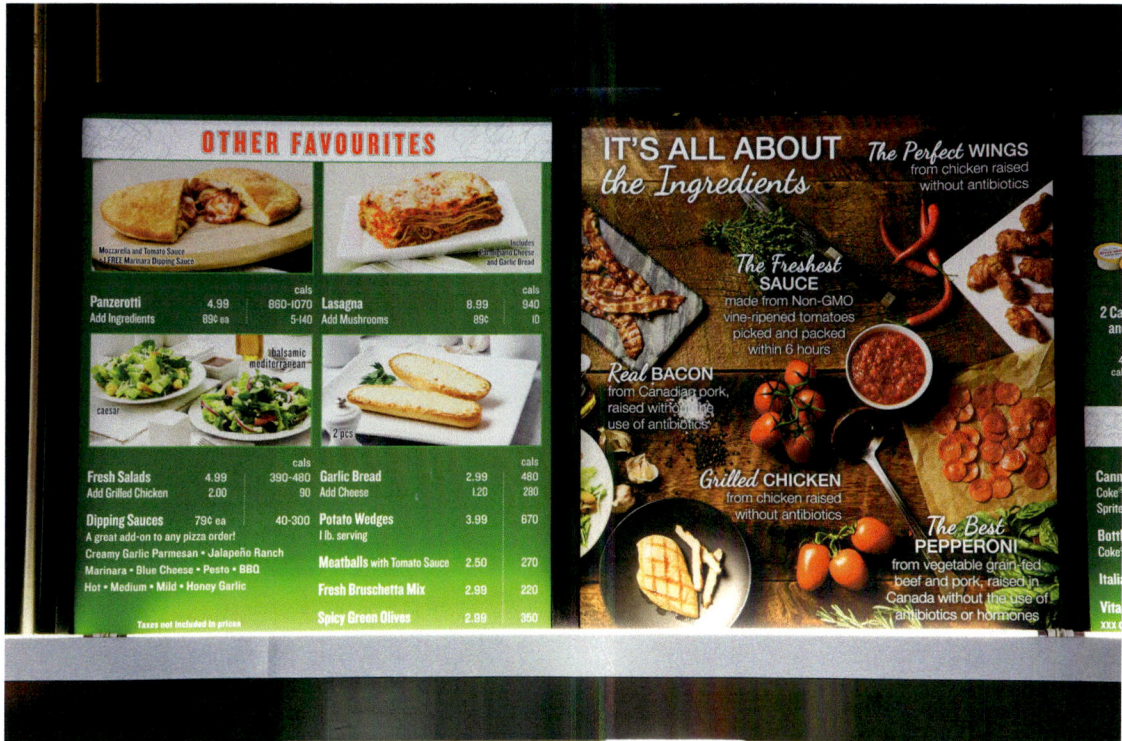

Pizza Nova's menu has grown to include sandwiches, salads, lasagna and more. Photo: Rick O'Brien

in the right way. If you order bacon for example, you want to put it on at the very end so the pizza crisps up. Training helps you understand what order to put the ingredients on the pizza and ensures everyone's doing it the same way.

The franchising business model is unique because store operators are also business owners. How do you ensure buy-in across the organization—your employees, your franchisees, and their store-level staff?

[Domenic] Somebody who buys a franchise does so for a reason. They like the brand, they like what you do. They're not looking to take the kinds of risks a typical entrepreneur is willing to take. They're looking for our expertise to help them. So it's up to us, it's our job to make sure they're successful.

We're talking to our franchisees all the time, and getting together as a group three or four times a year. We're constantly getting feedback, sharing information about where the market's going, talking about ways to improve product and services.

When we did a corporate exercise a few years ago to come up with our core values as an organization, we got everybody involved, from our office to our call centre to the franchisees.

That's our mentality, that's how we do business. We call it the family. It's not just our immediate family—the people who work with us and our franchisees are part of the extended family. Once a year we go out of town with our franchisees and their families. The families enjoy the amenities of the hotel while we have a half day general meeting. Then at night we have a gala and give out awards.

It's our way of saying thank you to people who are out in the trenches, people who sometimes

The Primucci line of imported products are part of the evolution of the Pizza Nova brand. Photo: Rick O'Brien

have to sacrifice time with their families to get the business going. When you win an award in front of your family, it makes it all worthwhile.

COMPANY VALUES AND THE FUTURE OF PIZZA

Technology plays a big role in the pizza industry. How has it affected Pizza Nova in particular?

[Domenic] I make the joke sometimes that we've become a technology company selling pizza. Even though the majority of our orders are still by phone, more and more are happening electronically every year.

You have to constantly invest in technology to keep up, to give customers the option of interacting with you however they want. We've updated our website four or five times since it launched because we see it as an aspect of good customer service: to give people a simple, positive experience whether they buy from us in person, over the phone, or online.

Are there any trends you see today that you think will have a lasting effect on the industry?

There are so many it's hard to keep track. But we're not really a company that follows trends. However we do believe there's a shift going on in the marketplace, especially amongst younger customers, and I'd say we're leading in this space. It's the demand for foods raised without antibiotics. There's a lot of talk about it these days, with people looking for healthier products.

When we decided to start making a shift ourselves a number of years ago, we said, let's start with our number one topping, which was pepperoni. But it took us a year to do. Because our supplier had to ensure that the farms had enough supply for us to make a permanent change—not just our needs today, but next year and the following one, as we continue to grow.

In this regard I think we have a bit of an advantage over some of our competitors. We're big enough that our suppliers are willing to work with us to make these kinds of changes. But because we're a mid-sized company (over 140 locations) we can move a little more quickly than some bigger companies. Because not all farms have changed, and some never will.

But there's demand in the marketplace. So in the past few years we've added four more proteins—our chicken wings, grilled chicken, bacon, and ham. Again we don't really follow trends but we believe today people really want to know what's in their food. They want information about allergens, nutritional facts, sustainability. And they're also looking for who you are as a company, what you do in the community, are you giving back.

[Sam] We're very proud of the work we've done with organizations like Variety Village and Easter Seals, for many years. We don't go out and advertise these things. It's not marketing; it's giving back to the community.

Just lately we started a breakfast program. Do you know how many thousands of kids go to school without having breakfast? So we have a little box at every store for our breakfast program.

Domenic, you've talked about the commodification of pizza in the food market today. What do you mean by that, and how does it affect your business?

Our industry has evolved enormously since we opened in 1963. Pizza started out as a snack food, now it's a lunch or a dinner too. But ad-

Photo: Rick O'Brien

ditionally, as a product, it's almost becoming a commodity. You can find pizza anywhere now: supermarkets make fresh pizza on site—90% of restaurants sell pizzas these days. So the question is, how do we stay relevant under those circumstances?

That's why you have to keep evolving: over 30 toppings; offering products without antibiotics; better service; and so on. We have to keep carving out our niche at the higher end of the delivery pizza market if we want to stay competitive down the road.

FOOTNOTE

[1] "Pizza Nova's Recipe for Growth," Financial Post, Rick Spence, July 17, 2015.

What Is True Neapolitan Pizza?

Neapolitan pizza has no inventors, no fathers, no masters,
but is the fruit of the creativity of the Neapolitan people.
—*AVPN President Antonio Pace*

Pizza Napoletana or Neapolitan pizza is a traditional speciality guaranteed (TSG) product, which means that it's officially recognized by the European Union as a dish of cultural and historical significance. The designation is meant to protect the special character of the product—how it's made, and the primary ingredients used—by distinguishing it from other similar products.

As we've seen in previous chapters, there are many types of pizza that have evolved from the original pizza napoletana: some directly, like New York pizza, and some indirectly, like New Haven-style pizza, a variation on the New York style. Today some of these styles are globally known and of historic significance themselves.

The certification of Neapolitan pizza as a TSG product is the result of the work of the Associazione Verace Pizza Napoletana (AVPN, or The True Neapolitan Pizza Association), a non-profit organization that was founded in Naples in 1984. At first there were just 17 members, all traditional Neapolitan pizzeria owners like Vincenzo and Antonio Pace, father and son founders of the AVPN, and proprietors of Ciro a Santa Brigida, a family business whose origins date back to the 19th century.

Pace, the long-time president of the AVPN, says that the increasing misuse of terms like "original pizza napoletana" in the fast- and frozen-food sectors was a catalyst for creating the group in 1984. But he is quick to add that the organization was created to affirm the Neapolitan tradition rather than denounce others that have followed.

ORIGINS OF THE AVPN

"Imagine that at the beginning of the 1950s there were maybe six or seven pizzerias outside of Naples," says Pace. "Whereas by the 1980s there were more than 2,500. But everyone was doing their own thing; nobody followed the rules."

Close-up of the Margherita Pizza at Toronto's Viva Napoli. Photo: Rick O'Brien

Photo: Ciro a Santa Brigida

"I felt I needed to intervene in some way or the real pizza napoletana would eventually disappear."

Pace realized that in order to defend the recipe he first had to create it—because until this time it only existed as loose association of family recipes, most of them passed down orally from one generation to the next. And of course these recipes varied slightly from one pizzeria to the next.

Notwithstanding a fair degree of skepticism he managed to bring together *le vecchie famiglie*—the oldest pizzerias in the city—and together with the help of a notary they agreed on a simple recipe that could work as a guideline for anyone wanting to learn the traditional way of making pizza napoletana.

"We wanted to achieve something simple," he says, "a recipe where a pizzaiolo with a watch and a scale could make a good pizza. As for excellence, that only comes with experience."

Encouraged by their initial success, the Asso-

ciation continued to evolve and refine its rules and regulations over the years. By 2009, in collaboration with the University of Naples and the Naples Chamber of Commerce, the AVPN successfully lobbied the European Union for protected status for pizza napoletana. It was the first time a food of its kind had received such a designation.

"Before this it was only wines and cheeses that were given DOP status. Today there are many other kinds of foods: breads, gelatos, and so on. But we were the first," says Pace.

Membership has grown exponentially since then, first within Italy and then beyond. Today there are 670 AVPN members across the globe in 38 different countries. The Association also runs a state-of-the-art training, testing and development facility in Naples, as well as satellite training facilities in Los Angeles and Osaka.

"The United States has the greatest number of members outside of Italy, followed by Japan," says Pace. "Recently there's been a great interest

The Association performs rigorous, periodic checks on all of its members to ensure those using the brand name are following the traditional methods outlined below.

Official AVPN guidelines

in places like Mexico, Sao Paolo and Australia as well."

Today AVPN's mandate includes:

• Training for pizza makers, beginner to master level
• Compliance: upholding regulations amongst members and approved suppliers
• Research and development for new products and approaches, e.g. gluten-free pizza.

THE CHARACTERISTICS OF PIZZA NAPOLETANA

Today, thanks to the AVPN and its followers, pizza Napoletana is very well documented. Here's how the APVN describe the finished product in its official guidelines:

"The consistency of the "Verace Pizza Napoletana" should be soft, elastic, easy to manipulate and fold. The centre should be particularly soft to the touch and taste, where the red of the tomato is evident, and to which the oil or—for the Pizza Marinara—the green of the oregano and the white of the garlic has perfectly amalgamated. In the case of the Pizza Margherita, the white of the mozzarella should appear in evenly spread patches, with the green of the basil leaves, slightly darkened by the cooking process."

The crust should deliver the flavour of well-prepared, baked bread. This mixed with the slightly acidic flavour of the densely enriched

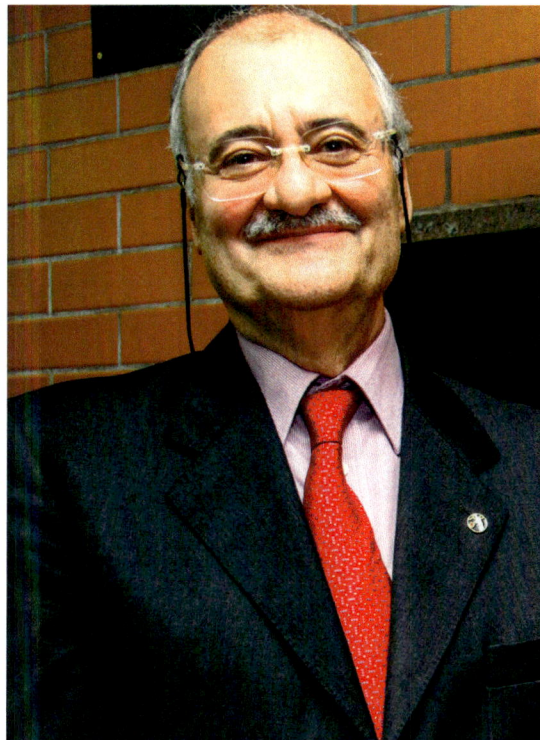

AVPN President Antonio Pace. Photo: Ciro a Santa Brigida

ORIGINAL MEMBERS OF THE AVPN

Ciro a Santa Brigida
Mattozzi a Piazza Carità
Don Salvatore
Al Ragno D'Oro
Lombardi a Santa Chiara
Salvatore alla Riviera
Ciro al Borgo Marinari
Alba
Cafasso
Marino
Rocco e i suoi Fratelli
Solo Pizza
De Vito
Vittoria
Capasso
Lombardi a Foria
Gianni al Vesuvio

71

Viva Napoli owner Giustino Iorio. Photo: Rick O'Brien

tomatoes, and the respective aroma of oregano and garlic or basil and the cooked mozzarella ensures that the pizza, as it emerges from the oven, delivers its characteristic aroma—perfumed and fragrant.

AVPN member Giustino Iorio, second generation Neapolitan restaurateur and owner of Viva Napoli in Toronto, says a defining characteristic of the pizza is the way it melts in your mouth:

The centre may even seem undercooked to some people, but to a Neapolitan pizza aficionado is just right. It melts in your mouth—si squaglia in bocca we say in Italian. Fans of Da Michele in Naples will line up a long time just to get a Margherita che si squaglia in bocca.

VARIETIES

There are two officially recognized varieties of pizza napoletana: marinara and margherita.

Pizza marinara is the older of the two varieties, dating back to the early 18th century. The name means "seafarer's pizza" because it was popular amongst sailors and fishermen who would buy them in the morning to take out to sea. The simplicity of the recipe made it perfect for the men to pack for later consumption: peeled San Marzano tomatoes, garlic, oregano, sea salt, and extra virgin olive oil.

Pizza margherita (discussed in chapter 2) was invented in 1889 by a pizzaiolo named Rafaele Esposito, who named it after Queen Margherita of Savoia after she sampled his recipe and expressed her approval. The pizza is topped with peeled San Marzano tomatoes, fresh mozzarella di bufala or fior di latte, (optional) grated hard cheese—usually aged pecorino, fresh basil, and extra virgin olive oil

The fact that there are only two traditional varieties has led many people outside of Naples to wrongly assume that the use of other toppings is somehow erroneous or inauthentic. Pace says that is not the case.

"My grandfather, who had a pizzeria at the beginning of the twentieth century, made 24 different styles of pizza. A pizza bianca, a mar-

Centennial College student making Pizza Marinara.
Photo: Victor Virgilio

The Margherita Pizza from the place that invented it: Pizzeria Brandi

Certified Neapolitan pizza topped with Ontario prosciutto at Pizzeria Libretto. Photo: Rick O'Brien

inara with mussels or anchovies, a margherita with mushrooms or prosciutto—none of these pizzas were exceptional or out of the ordinary in the least," says Pace.

"In fact, when I was a child people would be shopping at the fishmonger or deli and then come to the pizzeria and ask us to make a pizza with whatever they had bought."

"For us, the real pizza napoletana is a disk of dough. It's the way it's leavened, how the dough is formed, the soft centre, the raised cornicione. And always eaten *al libretto*, folded in four."

CONSISTENCY

Compared with other styles of pizza in North America and Italy, pizza napoletana is soft and malleable, somewhat similar to Indian naan bread.

THICKNESS

By international standards pizza napoletana is relatively thin, but it's thicker than many of the popular Italian styles of pizza. AVPN guidelines stipulate it should be no more than 0.4 cm at its centre, with a characteristic *cornicione* (raised peripheral frame or crust) of 1-2 cm. The cornicione is light and airy, browned but not burned.

SIZE

Unlike typical North American pizzas that are meant to be shared, pizza napoletana is always made in individual-sized portions. 35 cm (14 inches) is the maximum permitted circumference, made from a ball of dough weighing 180-250 mg.

AVPN certified pizza napoletana flour from 5 Stagioni

INGREDIENTS AND TOPPINGS

Like all Italian certified food products, pizza napoletana TSG has specific guidelines and technical parameters for products that can be used for its dough and toppings.

FLOUR

00 flour, made from soft wheat and known in Italian as *doppio zero,* is the primary flour used for making pizza napoletana. 00 is the most refined of all flours—pure white, and free of bran or wheat germ. It's a medium strength flour, which means its protein and gluten levels are moderate. For this reason, a small amount (maximum 20%) of type 0 flour, a wheat flour known as *Manitoba* in Italian, may be also used. Manitoba is a strong flour (technically over 400 W), and is used to add elasticity to the dough, which is sometime necessary due to temperature or humidity.

WATER

Pizza napoletana dough does not contain fat and is made with 60% water, less than many other doughs, like pizza romana. Yet it's soft and moist because it's cooked at such a high temperature and for such a short time (60-90 seconds), essentially flash-cooking the dough.

YEAST

The standard is naturally produced compressed yeast (*saccharomyces cerevisiae*), low in acidity. However mother yeast (or sourdough starter) is also permitted.

SALT

Fine sea salt (*sale marino fino*) is the sole type of salt permitted.

TOMATOES

Outside of Campania, canned peeled tomatoes are used for topping pizza napoletana, and San Marzano DOP are the gold standard recommended by the APVN. But in Campania itself you'll find either fresh or canned, depending on the establishment and the season. When fresh tomatoes are used, it's typically crudo—i.e. uncooked, placed on the pizza after it is cooked.

The AVPN specifies three varieties of fresh tomatoes that can be used, all grown in the province of Salerno, just south of Mount Vesuvius. The first and most famous variety is San Marzano dell'Agro Sarnese-Nocerino DOP. San Marzano tomatoes are fleshier and sweeter than Roma tomatoes and have a longer growing season, making them ideal for commercial production. To be classified as San Marzano DOP tomatoes must be produced within the Agro Sarnese Noc-

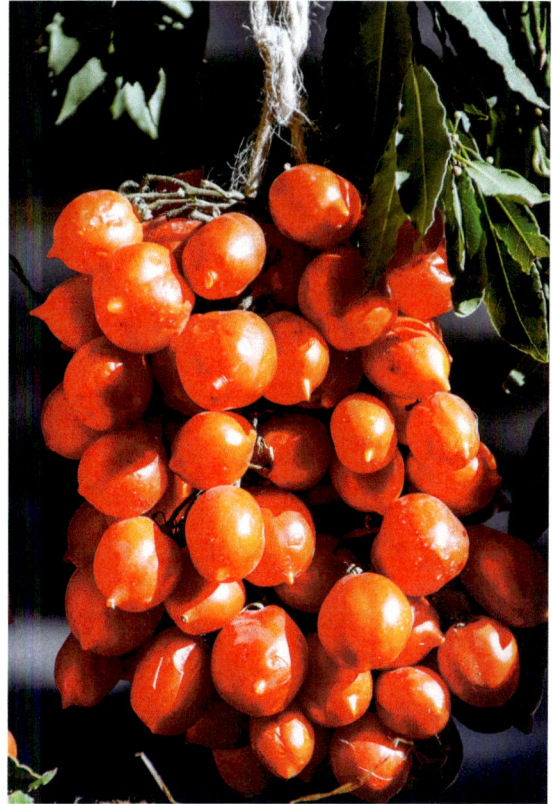
Pomodorini del Piennolo del Vesuvio

Mozzarella di Bufala by Quality Cheese, Vaughan ON.
Photo: Rick O'Brien

75

erino area of Salerno.

Another officially recognized variety is *Pomodorino del Piennolo del Vesuvio DOP*, a sweet, fiery red grape tomato grown in various communes in Mount Vesuvius National Park. Also known as *pomodorino vesuviano*, this variety is oblong in shape and about a quarter the size of a San Marzano tomato (25-30g). The name *piennolo* derives from *pendolo* (pendulum), a reference to the way these tomatoes are woven together and hung in the open air, to be preserved throughout the winter months.

The final official APVN-recognized tomato variety is *pomodorino di Corbara*, or *Corbarino*, a small, pear-shaped fruit cultivated in the hills of Corbara, a small commune to the north of Mount Lattari. This heritage variety dates back centuries but has only recently become available outside the Corbara area. Pomodorino di Corbara reflects the particular characteristics of the volcanic soil of the Lattari slopes, which gives it its high sugar content and "sweet and sour" taste.

Outside of Campania, peeled plum tomatoes are sometimes used but they must meet the technical parametres set out by the APVN. The APVN also has a strict rule against the use of genetically modified (GMO) tomatoes of any kind—whether for aesthetic purposes, pest resistance, or increased crop yield.

MOZZARELLA DI BUFALA

The production of *mozzarella di bufala* dates back over 1,000 years in Campania, long before a similar cheese was made from cow's milk rather than buffalo. Today it is made in various regions across Italy, but the official DOP variety—the one used to make pizza margherita—is restricted to seven provinces in the Lazio and Campania regions: Caserta, Salerno, Benevento, Naples, Frosinone, Latina, and Rome.

Fior di latte by Quality Cheese. Photo: Rick O'Brien

Prized for its high fat and casein content, mozzarella di bufala is a fresh cheese, meant to be consumed within a few days after it is produced.

FIOR DI LATTE

A more recently invented form of mozzarella, *fior di latte* is made from cow's milk that dates back several centuries and is also believed to have originated in Campania. It is lighter in taste and less fatty than mozzarella di bufala, but its production method and shelf life are virtually the same. Fior di latte is an AVPN-accepted substitute for *mozzarella di bufala*.

HARD CHEESE

Some establishments will add a sprinkle of hard cheese (up to 15g) to their pizza margherita to

The formation of the balls ('panetti') must be done exclusively by hand. This technique, known as 'staglio a mano,' where the dough is made into small balls called 'panetti', is reminiscent of the technique used in the preparation of mozzarella—'mozzatura'—also done by hand.

Official AVPN Guidelines

School of Italian Pizza instructor Bruno Di Sarno mixes the dough; covers it with a wet cloth to ferment; hand cuts, shapes and weighs the panetti. Photos: Rick O'Brien

enhance its flavour profile. Aged pecorino, made from sheep's milk, is most commonly used, but parmigiano reggiano is also permitted.

OLIVE OIL

AVPN guidelines call for the use of extra virgin or virgin olive oil because of its resistance to high temperatures, which can cause certain types of oil to oxidize. This "smoke point" —the temperature at which an oil starts to burn—is important from both a taste and a health perspective. Burning oil destroys its healthy properties (like the polyphenols in olive oil) and can even be harmful to your health.

HERBS

The use of dried oregano and fresh basil to top flatbreads of various kinds go backs to antiquity in Italy, long before in the invention of pizza. Oregano, paired with garlic, is the primary herb used for pizza marinara, though many pizzaioli will finish with a touch of basil. In the case of pizza margherita, basil is the only herb used: no additional or substitute herbs are permitted.

MAKING THE DOUGH

Preparing the Napoletana pizza dough is a multi-step process that comprises mixing the ingredients, proofing the dough in two stages, and finally forming the *disco di pasta* (disk of dough).

- Flour, water, salt, and yeast are combined in a mixer to achieve desired consistency.
- Dough is mixed at low speed, eventually forming a ball of optimal consistency: sticky, soft, elastic "to the touch" (known in Italian as the *punto di pasta*). It is important at this stage to ensure the water is completely absorbed and the dough does not become warm.

FERMENTATION - 2 STAGES

- The dough is removed from the mixer and set aside to rise for two hours. It is covered by a wet cloth to prevent hardening or the formation of a crust.
- The dough is hand-cut into pieces weighing between 180-250g and shaped into balls. These

Lightly dusting the work surface; removing proofed panetti from dough box. Photos: Rick O'Brien

Working the air out to form the cornicione; topping the pizza in a centrifugal motion. Photo: Rick O'Brien

The base must be prepared by hand. The pizzaiolo's skill enables him or her to determine the movement of air in the base ensuring it moves from the centre towards the periphery, thus forming the frame or crust known as 'cornicione.' No other type of preparation is acceptable ... Specifically excluded is the use of a rolling pin and mechanical presses.

Official AVPN Guidelines

Using a spoon, place the pressed, peeled tomatoes into the centre of the pizza base, then using a spiralling motion, cover the entire surface of the base with the sauce excluding the crust... Using a traditional copper oil canister and the same spiralling motion, starting from the centre and moving out, pour Extra Virgin Olive Oil/Olive oil over the pizza.

Official AVPN Guidelines

Gently stretching the dough; topping it with extra virgin olive oil from a copper canister. Photo: Rick O'Brien

panetti are then set in special dough proofing containers to rise an additional 4-6 hours.

FORMING THE PIZZA

After the second rising the panetti are ready for baking. The pizzaiolo lightly dusts a work area with flour and places the ball of risen dough on it.

Working quickly and fluidly to avoid sticking, the pizzaiolo gently works the air of the dough out from the centre to the periphery, forming the characteristic cornicione of the pizza napoletana.

TOPPING THE PIZZA

Beginning and ending with the classic centrifugal swirl, the pizzaiolo layers on the hand-crushed tomato and other ingredients before finishing with a 4-5g shot of extra virgin olive oil.

BAKING THE PIZZA

With a lightly-floured wood or aluminum peel the pizzaiolo transfers the pizza onto the stone cooking plain of a wood-burning oven heated to 485° C or 905° F. Thanks to a skillful flick of the wrist the condiment remains undisturbed.

Because of the high heat and rapid cooking time (60-90 seconds) the pizzaiolo must continually monitor the pizza, rotating it often to ensure it is cooked consistently.

The Alleanza at 50 Kalò di Ciro Salvo: fior di latte, lardo, red onion, conciato romano cheese. Photo: 50 Kalò

The tomato should have lost all excess water, and should be dense and consistent; the mozzarella di bufala DOP or the mozzarella STG should have melted on the surface of the pizza; the basil, garlic, and oregano will develop an intense aroma, and will appear brown, but not burned.

Official AVPN Guidelines

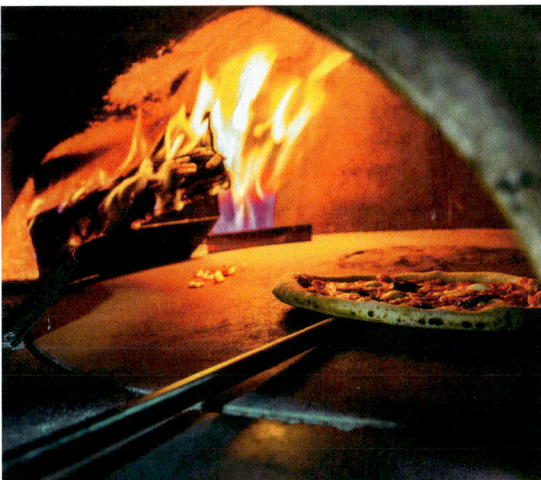

Bruno Di Sarno with peel and spinner; dusting the peel and sliding on the pizza; spinning the pizza and removing when cooked. Photo: Rick O'Brien

THE ART OF NEOPOLITAN PIZZA MAKING

The pizza secret lies all in the dough rising. Its recipe? It doesn't exist and I can tell you that, because I've learnt since I was a child that dough rising changes according to the weather, hot or cold, dry or damp. For instance if it's cold, you need hot water and a little salt; if it's hot you need less salt since it slows down the rising. These issues must be taken into consideration the night before, when preparing the dough. Ten to twelve hours are needed for a perfect rising. You can standardize the process, but it is the experience that refines the art. —Vincenzo Pace

For all its guidelines and technical requirements, making pizza napoletana is as much an art form as it is a science. As Vincenzo Pace, one of the architects of the APVN himself says, there's no substitute for experience: essential knowledge gained slowly, over time, through trial and error is what "refines the art" of pizza making.

It's partly about adjusting yeast and salt levels and water temperatures to account for fluctuations in room temperature and humidity. The strength of the yeast or flour can also vary. Then there's the precise, manual process of forming the disco di pasta, which is done quickly to avoid sticking, using as little flour as possible to avoid a bitter aftertaste. And finally the extreme heat and speed of the baking process is taken into account: the continual manoeuvring and rotating of each pizza so it's cooked thoroughly and evenly in less than 90 seconds, and carefully keeping it in the same spot on the cooking plain to avoid burning.

"Making the dough requires the pizzaiolo's constant attention," says Giustino Iorio. "For all its simplicity, it's actually very technical. It's not something that can really be explained. It's something that comes from trial and error, peo-

Vincenzo Iorio slides a classic Pizza Margherita into Viva Napoli's Stefano Ferrara wood oven. Photo: Rick O'Brien

ple making pizza over and over again, with a Neapolitan pizza chef who is overlooking, correcting, giving suggestions. In Naples, to be a respected pizza chef, you have to being doing it full time for at least three years, otherwise you're still a novice." Iorio first learned about the craft growing up in Naples as a close friend of the Leone family, owners of the storied Trianon de Ciro, and perfected his pizzaiolo training under the guidance APVN's Peppe Miele.

When Iorio's own son, Vincenzo, expressed interest in the pizza maker's trade, Giustino brought in a pizzaiolo from Naples for him to train under for his first year.

"Every day it's a bit different because of the different temperature or humidity," says Vincenzo. "In some ways it's harder to make a consistently great pizza here in Toronto than in Naples because the weather changes more drastically."

Under the Neapolitan pizzaiolo's tutelage he became more keenly aware of subtle sensory cues that the seasoned pizza maker employs in the pursuit of the perfect dough.

"I know how it tastes just by looking at it in the oven, seeing how the dough reacts to the heat," says Vincenzo. "And the punto di pasta, the feel of the dough, that's what it's all about for the Neapolitan pizza maker. To achieve that punto di pasta is a little different every day because of a million little things."

The final critical thing from Giustino's perspective is the palate, something he acquired as a native of Naples and his son acquired spending his summers there when he was growing up.

"The palate for the Neapolitan pizza is a must and that comes from spending time there, eating it over and over and over again. Unless you have that, it doesn't matter who's trained you, you cannot do the true product," he says. "If the pizzaiolo doesn't have the acquired palate, just like a sommelier would have from years of tasting, or nose if you're a cheese critic."

The Parmigiana di Melanzane (eggplant parmesan) is one of Viva Napoli's signature pizzas. Photo: Rick O'Brien

Luca di Massa, +39 Italian Food

Guglielmo Vuolo, Eccelenze Campane

Paolo Surace, I Mattozzi

Luca di Massa, owner of +39 Italian Food, a Neapolitan pizzeria in Bologna:

"I advise you to follow your instincts and never forget the two main ingredients of pizza neapoletana: tradition and passion."

Paolo Surace, son of AVPN Vice-President and co-founder, whose family pizzeria I Mattozzi dates back to the 1800s:

"Often during my courses or workshops around the world, I get asked for advice on how to choose good flour. The first thing is to study and have a clear idea of the finished product you want to achieve. I say this because there's no miraculous flour that standardizes our craft or makes it easy—we are artisans."

Guglielmo Vuolo, fourth generation pizzaiolo and owner of Eccelenze Campane in Naples:

"I think it's the duty of a craftsman to face the challenge of a new flour. Understand how to take it and get what you want from it.

The advice I give to my students is to always put passion first. The professionalism you acquire through experience and humility naturally leads to experimentation, but you should always seek to defend the consistency of your approach and align yourself with the needs of consumers. Personally I look for products that give me a sense of a forgotten flavour, because I believe in old things you always find something new."

Gino Sorbillo, third generation pizza maker, former winner of the Campionato della Pizza Napoletana.

Gino Sorbillo using Alitalia Pizzolivm, an olive oil blend designed for pizza makers.

"My approach is to work with the true identity of products, to always strive to improve, and collaborate with high quality producers.

We pizzaioli and chefs are lucky today compared to the past. Our producers aren't just some companies advertising their products in a magazine. They work directly with us, side-by-side, as part of the team. They're competent, intelligent men and women who like us respect tradition but also want to build on it, get better every day."

A young Enzo Coccia. Photos courtesy of Enzo Coccia.

Un Maestro Pizzajuolo

Interview With Master Pizza Maker Enzo Coccia

For those who follow the restaurant scene in Italy, especially anyone with a passion for pizza, Enzo Coccia is a household name. The third generation pizzajuolo ("pizza maker" in the Neapolitan dialect) is regularly featured in the Italian food press and has also received coverage internationally in publications like *Le Monde, The Daily Telegraph* and *The New York Times*.

A man in his mid-fifties with the verve of someone half his age, Coccia owns and operates three pizzerias on Via Michelangelo da Caravaggio in Naples: La Notizia 53, La Notizia 94, and O' Sfizio d''a Notizia. He is also the founder of the professional training agency Pizza Consulting and the co-author of the book *"Pizza Napoletana: A Scientific Guide About the Artisanal Process."*

In 2009, Coccia collaborated with the Associazione Verace Pizza Napoletana and the University of Naples Federico II in their successful bid for EU certification of pizza napoletana. Pizza Napoletana TSG (Traditional Speciality Guaranteed) is now a registered geographical mark that protects European pizzerias who make their products in adherence to the traditional recipe.

Gambero Rosso's Annual Pizzerie d'Italia has consistently ranked Coccia's pizzerias in its Tre Spicchi top-in-class category (the highest possible designation) since it began in 2013. And when a group of food critics led by Luciano Pignataro recently compiled their own "Top 50" list of Italian pizzerias, Coccia's La Notizia 94 was chosen fourth best in the country. He was also given a special alla Carriera (Lifetime Achievement) award by the group, in recognition of his many accomplishments over the past four decades.

Congratulations on winning the lifetime achievement award at the inaugural 50 Top Pizza. How did it feel?

Interior of Pizzeria La Notizia 94 with poster from the film Citizen Kane.

Thank you very much, it was very moving. I have been very fortunate in my life, for two reasons. The first is that my father made me study, that has been extremely important for me. The other is that in the past 15 years, the business of pizza has experienced a big boom. When I started 36 years ago as a teenager, pizzerias were poor—nothing like today. Now there's a lot of money being invested in pizza all over the world.

Tell us about your background and how you got into the pizza business.

I was one of 10 children and my father (like my grandfather) owned the pizzeria Fortuna in the old city centre of Naples. From a very young age I was enchanted by the trade.

You have to recall that the pizzaiolo's counter in the pizzeria is a little elevated. He stands on a platform, so he oversees and commands the room. As a kid I watched my father—like a giant!—performing this magic, making a pizza in less than a minute! It was a beautiful thing that fascinated me. My dream was always to climb up there and make pizzas. But it took many years.

In 1994 you opened your first pizzeria and called it La Notizia (The News), an unusual name for a traditional pizzeria. Why did you choose it?

The thing you have to understand is that in those days I was fascinated with the director Orson Welles. He was a genius! He made me appreciate many things, like the importance of communications and the press, the power of how and where information is put.

In Citizen Kane, the protagonist says: "If the headline is big enough, it makes the news big enough." That's what I wanted to do with my pizza: put it on the first page, make it important!

People wait in line for hours outside a great pizzeria. This gives me immense satisfaction, it fills me with a feeling of joy. But it's important to always have respect—respect for the customers;

for the primary ingredients; for the work; for the collaborators; for the environment (something we have not done well I'm afraid).

Art seems to be an important influence on your ideas and the design of your pizzerias, which you sometime refer to as "PizzArias."

Yes, I am very passionate about the arts and history. Napoli is a beautiful city full of culture and museums, and I try to do whatever I can to preserve the history of my city. In fact, we made a pizza called the Capodimonte with provola di bufala, pomodori San Marzano a pacchetelle, salsiccia di bufala and pecorino romano. A dollar for every one of these pizzas we sell goes to the Capodimonte Museum, a very important museum in Naples, to help pay for the restoration of the works of Vincenzo Gemito, a great Neapolitan artist of the nineteenth century. We have raised over 500,000 euros so far!

In 2010 you opened a second pizzeria—also called La Notizia. But the approach was quite different, featuring non-traditional toppings like burrata, baccalà in cassuola, or lemon and bresaola. Why did you decide to go this route?

I think it's natural when you do any kind of creative work, whether you're making movies or making pizzas. Of course you have to master the basics first, that's fundamental. But then you evolve and grow, in your own personal way, through research and experimentation. You need to challenge yourself to keep growing. That's what I did!

That's why in 2010 I opened La Notizia 94 in the same street of the first La Notizia, that changed the name into La Notizia 53 because of the street number. La Notizia 94 represents my authentic laboratory of creativity, where I try

Enzo Coccia today.

original combinations and new sensorial paths also with the addition of wines, spumanti and artisan beers.

At the same time we're still guided by classic principles. We are searching for the right balance of ingredients, using the highest quality materials, trying to strike an equilibrium between experimentation and tradition.

The Italian press often calls you the father of pizza gourmet. What are your thoughts on that?

I prefer to describe myself as an artisan of the pizza rather than the father of pizza gourmet. However, it's a great movement. When they say "Enzo Coccia is the father of pizza gourmet," and I think about what this new generation of pizzaioli have accomplished in just a few years, it makes me very proud!

La Notizia 94 is also known for the quality of its wine list, which is not that typical in Italy, where beer is the more common accompaniment to pizza. Do you think wine is actually a better pairing?

Obviously it depends on the taste of each one of us, but I suggest to drink wine with my pizzas. We have a good selection of artisanal beers as well, and that's a growing industry here in Italy, but beer is not the traditional drink here. Having beer with pizza is something we learned from the Americans during the Second World War. Historically it was wine that was drunk with a pizza, not something heavy but something light and citrusy like Falanghina, a grape that was born and has been grown in this area since ancient times.

La Notizia 94 was listed in the Michelin guide one year after it opened, in its "fork" category for quality of experience. What was the significance of this for you?

'Mpustarella panino from 'O Sfizio d'a Notizia

It was a great moment for me, I was very moved by this recognition, almost in tears when I heard about it. A pizzeria being recognized by the French! It signified that pizza had finally been accepted, as a unique dish—a legitimate and valuable cuisine.

Pizza Fritta dolce with buffalo ricotta and Sorrento lemon leaf.

In 2016 you opened your third Notizia—'O Sfizio d''a Notizia (The Whim of the News)—once again with a completely different approach than your previous work. This time the menu features fried rather than baked pizza, and a historic form of bread called 'mpustarella that you discovered in your research and reinvented for a twenty-first century audience.

In my most recent creation I tried to elevate two very popular Neapolitan dishes: the fried pizza and the 'mpustarella. People think of fried pizza as a street food for the poor, but it's an ancient dish of the people of Naples, even older than baked pizza.

At 'O Sfizio d''a Notizia the fried pizza is completely renewed and has become an elegant, soft and easy to digest food, and has now the potential to become another iconic dish from Naples.

What can you tell us about 'mpustarella?

'Mpustarella is another ancient food I discovered for the first time in an old poem. The original recipe is tough and heavy but through a long testing process I developed our own version that's light and soft and airy, but still has that rusticity and depth of flavour of the original. The panini are classics: mortadella and smoked mozzarella or curly escarole and salami.

The wine list at 'O Sfizio d''a Notizia is mostly sparkling—local and imported. What was your thinking here?

To combine an ancient tradition and more innovative and contemporary inspirations I try to select top quality products for my menu and only the best choice of sparkling wines, mostly Italian and French. I select this kind of wine also

Pizza Fritta salata with zucchini flowers.

because, especially in 'O Sfizio d''a Notizia, we prepare a lot of fried food and a sparkling wine is the best accompaniment because it cleans your palette.

The pizza industry has changed a great deal since you started three and half decades ago. Any thoughts on where it's going in the future?

Pizza Napoletana has a long tradition and without doubt it will continue to spread all over the world. 20 years ago it was hardly known outside of Italy, now there are many authentic Neapolitan pizzerias in US, Canada, Australia, Japan, even Brasil and I believe it will continue to grow for a long, long time.

It is an honour for me to be an ambassador of the original Pizza Napoletana. I was born in this reality and I will continue to make and teach this "art" as long as I can.

Varieties of Pizza

An Overview Of The Many Styles

In chapter 1 we looked at some of the many traditional flatbreads found across the Italian peninsula to show that pizza was just one member of a very large family—albeit the most famous one, by far.

But even that's a bit simplistic because pizza itself isn't one dish but many. It seems that every region or country across the globe that adopts pizza also adapts it in some way. It's an old tradition that began in 18th century Italy, continued in 19th century America, and continues in the 21st century around the world.

Here's an overview of the main varieties of pizza in the country that invented it, and the one that made it a global phenomenon after World War Two.

PIZZA IN ITALY [1]

PIZZA TONDA (ROUND PIZZA)

Pizza tonda, or *pizza tradizionale*, or just plain *pizza*, is the standard "pizzeria pizza" you'll find all over Italy. It's distinct from *pizza romana* or *napolitana* (described below) but derivative from those classic styles. It varies regionally: in the North it tends to be a little thicker and softer; in South and Central regions it gets a little thinner and crunchier* (*Agrodolce*).

Like its famous Roman and Neapolitan cousins, pizza tonda is typically made in individual-sized portions and is meant to be eaten fresh out of the oven, at the pizzeria. Pizza tonda is the perfect casual meal, firm enough to be eaten by hand without the need to fold *a portafoglio* as they do in Naples.

Like the other classic Italian styles, pizza tonda is baked directly on the floor (or cooking plain) of the oven, which these days is usually gas- or electric-powered rather than fire. Classic *condimenti* (toppings) include Margherita, Quattro Stagioni and Capricciosa (see chapter 6 for a full list of ingredients and toppings).

Pizza al taglio at Ciao Roma in Vaughan. Photo: Rick O'Brien

Classic pizza tonda (Italian style "round" pizza) at Terroni. Photo: Rick O'Brien

Pizza margherita at Viva Napoli. Photo: Rick O'Brien

Teamwork at Viva Napoli. Photo: Rick O'Brien

NAPOLETANA

Described in detail in previous chapters, pizza Napoletana is the oldest style of pizza and the most difficult to replicate.

It requires an oven that can reach 900° C or more, and traditionally one that is wood-burning, though gas ovens are becoming more common for cost and safety reasons

It also requires an expert pizzaiolo who can

- quickly form and dress the delicate disco di pasta
- slide it onto a peel and transfer it to the oven without spilling the toppings
- carefully rotate the pizza without shifting it on the oven floor (which causes burning)

This is all done within 2 to 3 minutes, hundreds of times per night at popular Neapolitan pizzerias. Little wonder pizzaioli often work in small teams, relay-style during peak hours.

PIZZA FRITTA AND CALZONE

Although we typically think of pizza as a baked flatbread with tomato and other condiments on top, pizza fritta and calzone, two varieties of pizza ripiena (stuffed pizza), play important roles in the history of Neapolitan pizza.

Stuffed dishes of this kind could be found as early as the 1500s in Naples, when zeppulelle were fried in oil and doused in honey. By the nineteenth century the duke Ippolito Cavalcanti describes a savoury fried pizza, stuffed with cod, blue fish and anchovies, in his treaty Cucina teorica-pratica (Theory and Practice of Cooking).

Classic Neapolitan calzone by Bruno Di Sarno at The School of Italian Pizza. Photo: Rick O'Brien

Pizza Fritta by Enzo Coccia

But in the modern era pizza fritta (fried pizza) has a strong association with post World War II Naples. The city was in crisis at the time, physically and economically devastated by the war. Wood, baking ovens, fresh cheese, tomatoes—the essential tools and ingredients to make a classic pizza napoletana—were hard to come by and too expensive for the average citizen.

During this period it was common to see women preparing and selling fried pizzas outside their family homes. They were often sold a ogge a otto, meaning on credit, with payment due within eight days.

In recent years the pizza fritta has been rediscovered in cities across Italy. And like its famous cousin, pizza al forno (oven baked pizza) it has been elevated and reinvented by top Italian pizzaioili like Enzo Coccia and Gino Sorbillo.

By comparison calzone—a stuffed or "folded" baked pizza—is less distinct or conspicuous than pizza fritta. There's a practical reason for this of course: calzoni are baked in the same ovens as classic Neapolitan pizzas, whereas pizza fritta requires a deep-frier. That means an added cost for the pizzeria to buy and maintain this extra piece of equipment if they want to offer both products.

Calzone is a very common menu item found in traditional pizzerias of the Campania region. The panzerotto, originating from the neighbouring region of Puglia, is essentially the same dish, except there the same term is used to describe both fried or baked versions of the product.

ROMANA

Compared with pizza napoletana, pizza romana (Roman pizza) is light, thin, and noticeably crunchy. In fact Romans often refer to it as *la schrocchiarella*, which literally means "crunchy."

Pizza Fritta at Gino Sorbillo's Zia Esterina

The lightness of the pizza is due in part to the fact that it contains about a third less flour than pizza napoletana (160-180g versus 250g). There's also less water content because the pizza is cooked at a lower temperature for a longer period of time, which causes a higher degree of dehydration.

The dough for making pizza romana is pressed before baking, either by hand or by rolling pin, resulting in a cracker-thin dough with an almost non-existent crust. One final and import difference from pizza napoletana is the use of oil in the dough (olive or peanut are most commonly used), which gives the finished pizza a crunchier consistency.

Pizza romana is typically eaten with a fork and knife, or cut into small sections that are eaten by hand. And while it is traditionally made *tonda* style, today there are many restaurants that also make an *alla pala* version. Long and rectangular, cut into pieces for sharing, this type of pizza gets its name from the traditional wooden baker's paddle (pala) on which it is served.

Classic "schrocchiarella" style pizza Romana at Pizzeria Defina. Photo: Rick O'Brien

Pizza al taglio (displayed on a "pala") at Sud Forno Photo: Rick O'Brien

PIZZA AL TAGLIO OR PIZZA IN TEGLIA

When Italians do take-out pizza it's usually *pizza al taglio*—pizza slices cut to order and typically sold by weight rather than standard size (which is more common in North America). This style of pizza is also known as *pizza in teglia* (pan-baked pizza) because it is often prepared in large rectangular trays rather than directly on the floor of the oven.

Pizzerias that sell this kind of pizza often have display cases accessible from the street so patrons can grab a slice on the go without ever setting foot inside the pizzeria.

Pizza in teglia dough is a little thicker and more hydrated than other styles of Italian pizza, making it ideal for reheating; in fact, some people think it tastes better that way than fresh out of the oven.

Gabrielle Bonci and his world-famous pizza romana, known its lightness, hydration and digestibility. Photo: Bonci

In the 1990s a version of pizza al taglio emerged in Rome, thanks to Gabriele Bonci and others. Sometimes call *teglia romana*, it's characterized by a high level of dough hydration, long periods of levitation, and experimentation with healthier types of grain.

Pizza in teglia romana is characteristically light, airy, crunchy, and digestible, and its popularity has grown throughout Italy and around the world. In fact, outside of Italy when establishments advertise "Roman-style pizza" it's typically teglia romana, not traditional Roman-style pizza, that they are serving.

Pizza romana sliced being heated up at Ciao Roma. Photo: Rick O'Brien

PIZZA GOURMET [2]

Once considered a lowly street food (literally and figuratively), pizza (and its purveyors) are now the subject of scholarly works, culinary guides and tours, and mainstream food media in Italy, often discussed in the same breath as the country's top restaurants and wines. The pizza gourmet movement has played an important role in the evolution of public perception.

Pizza gourmet is not a style of pizza but a loosely connected set of approaches to it. Enzo Coccia, who has been called the father of the movement, has tried to characterize it by breaking down its parts:

• Experimentation with a wide variety of **flours**: organic, whole wheat, Kamut, rice, semolina, grano antico, wheat germ, cricket, and hemp.

• Sourcing of **non-traditional toppings** with a strong emphasis on seasonal, regional, high quality, cleanly produced foods, and surprising, innovative combinations.

• The use of diverse **leavening agents**: brewer's yeast, mother yeast, dried mother yeast, biga; the "poolish" method (adapted from Polish breadmaking); autolyse, and no-yeast dough.

• Testing non-traditional **ingredients in the dough**: sea water, beer, whey, and vegetable carbons.

• Advancements in the **fermentation process**: 30 years ago, a 2-3 hour proofing was the commercial norm. Many have evolved to a 12-16 hour leavening period to produce

Verona-based Simone Padoan's I Tigli is one of Italy's most renowned gourmet pizzerias. It's "new concept" pizza combines haut cuisine with the highest quality artisanal baking techniques. Photos: I Tigli

"Summer Pizza" named after the Neapolitan song Torna a Surriento, by Enzo Coccia

a lighter, more digestible pizza. Today there are gourmet pizzerias experimenting with protracted "cold leavening" periods of up to 96 hours.

• Degustazione-style **presentation:** many pizza gourmet serve their pizzas on wooden cutting boards, cut into bite-sized pieces ideal for sharing, tapas-style.

• An emphasis on **wine and beer pairings**: artisanal beers, local and imported wines, spumanti, and even champagne are commonly found at gourmet pizzerias, though rarely at traditional ones.

Despite his importance to the pizza gourmet movement, Coccia has a healthy skepticism about many aspects of it, from the name ("it defines nothing") to some of its excessive practices.

"I'm in favour of well-researched, studious evolution, but exasperation—at that point I think we're just talking to ourselves" says Coccia. "I'll continue every night with the same dream: simply to make a good pizza. Or rather a great one. Nothing else."

BAKERY PIZZA

An overview of pizza in Italy would be incomplete without reference to bakery pizza, a popular snack food all over the peninsula.

The consistency and thickness of bakery pizza will vary from place to place, but it's typically made with oil or lard in the dough and a touch of sugar, giving the dough a moist texture and crunchy exterior, with a sweetish aftertaste. Often served *rosso* with a simple topping of tomato and herbs, it is also quite commonly served *bianco*—entirely without tomato sauce.

In fact the most famous pizza bianca, which hails from Rome, goes back centuries, predating the use of tomato and blurring the line between focaccia and pizza—a confusion that does not bother locals in the least.

Right: Italian pizza bianca is often cut lengthwise and used for panini, like this one at Sud. Photo: Rick O'Brien

Pizza al taglio, focaccia barese and pizza bianca with rapini at Aida's Pine Valley. Photos: Rick O'Brien

"If you go to any bread bakery, you'll see that almost everyone will buy a loaf of bread and a piece of pizza bianca, either to eat right away, for a child's school snack or just to bring home in place of bread," says Rome-based writer and photographer Elvira Zilli. "Most owners tend to give a small free piece of pizza bianca to kids while their mothers are lined up to buy bread. I believe simplicity makes a good pizza, even if it's a plain white pizza, with just salt and oil, something Romans will never say no to!"

The invention of pizza bianca is one of those fortunate accidents of history, born of necessity at time when the city's *fornai* (bakers) made their bread in wood-burning ovens that were not equipped with thermometers. To test the temperature, they would toss a small, flattened dough into the oven.

PIZZA IN NORTH AMERICA [3]

NEW YORK

As described in chapter 2, New York is the original home of American-style pizza, created by Southern Italians who emigrated to the North Eastern US in the late 1900s. Gennaro Lombardi invented a coal-burning oven in 1905 and that was the standard for New York pizzerias until Ira Nevin invented the gas-burning oven after World War Two.

New York pizzas (or "pies" as they are often called in the US) are much bigger than Italian *pizze tonde*—18 inches or wider, cut into large, pliable slices that are typically folded in two and eaten by hand. The dough is relatively thin, approximately one quarter inch, with a raised cornicione around the outer edge of the crust.

New York style pizza at North of Brooklyn. Photo: Rick O'Brien

CHICAGO OR DEEP-DISH

Invented by Ike Sewell and Ric Riccardo in Chicago in 1943, deep-dish pizza is quite literally a "pizza pie." Typically baked in a round, deep pan, its toppings are applied in layers: first cheese, then vegetable and meat, and finally the tomato sauce.

The crust itself is about an inch in thickness but often appears greater because it's molded into the concave shape of the pan. Because of the height and density of the pie, Chicago-style pizza can take up to 45 minutes to bake.

Chicago style pizza at Toronto's Double D's. Photo: Rick O'Brien

SICILIAN OR GRANDMA

Sicilian pizza—an American adaptation of Sicilian Sfincione—is a large, rectangular pan pizza that has become quite popular in the North Eastern US over the past few decades. It's based on a kind of home-style pizza common in Italian immigrant households across North America.

Early versions were made with tomato sauce, onion, anchovies, and breadcrumbs, though today it is common for mozzarella to be added. Sicilian pizza is very thick—up to two inches—while a thinner, crispier version called Grandma Pizza is approximately 1 inch thick.

One of the distinctive things about this pizza is the placement of the sauce on top of the cheese—the opposite of New York pizza.

DETROIT

An interesting regional variation on the Sicilian style invented in Michigan in the 1950s, Detroit pizza is a thick, rectangular pizza baked in repurposed blue steel pans that were actually created to hold small automotive parts.

The distinct caramelized crust of a Detroit pizza results from the cheese being spread to the very edge of the crust. Just before it's done, the pizza is removed from the pan and finished directly on the floor of the oven, giving it a crispy exterior. The classic Detroit pizza is topped with pepperoni and a blend of mozzarella and brick cheeses, then baked, and topped with hot marinara sauce once it is cooked.

Detroit style pizza at the Descendant in Leslieville. Photo: Rick O'Brien

ST. LOUIS

Little known outside the region, St. Louis pizza is a cracker-thin, no-yeast pizza invented in the 1950s by one of two historic pizzerias: either Imo's or Farotto's, depending on which version of the story you believe.

St. Louis-Style Pizza. Photo: Lopez-Alt, J. Kenji

St. Louis pizza is peculiar for its use of Provel, a stretch-less, slightly smoky cheese invented in Wisconsin in the 1940s, specifically for use in the pizza industry. This style has many proponents and detractors, but there's no denying its uniqueness.

CALIFORNIA

Long before the pizza gourmet movement in Italy there was a gourmet pizza trend in California. It started in the early 1980s and is closely associated with figures like Alice Waters, Wolfgang Puck, Ed LaDou, and more recently, Nancy Silverton.

Waters was a long-time student of the French and Italian traditions of regional, seasonal cuisine, and applied these sensibilities to pizza when she opened Chez Panisse Café in 1980.

Grande Cheese is one of the few local places that make Italian Pizza Al Metro (metre-long pizza). Photo: Rick O'Brien

Baking her pizza in a wood oven (highly unusual at the time), she experimented with non-traditional toppings like duck confit, quails eggs, and mussels.

Around the same time Lou LaDou was doing his own experimentation at Prego in San Francisco, when he was discovered by Wolfgang Puck. The two would go on to collaborate on the seminal Spago before LaDou joined forces with Richard L. Rosenfeld and Larry S. Flax to found California Pizza Kitchen, which today boasts over 250 locations. At Spago, LaDou was known for toppings like smoked salmon, duck sausage, and crème fraîche; during his California Pizza Kitchen era, his most famous innovation was the barbeque chicken pizza.

With the popularization of the movement, however, the gourmet aspect has largely disappeared.

OTHER VARIETIES OF PIZZA

The topic of international pizza styles could fill a book on its own. On the next page are a few of the styles of global pizza you may come across in your travels.

FOOTNOTES

[1] Descriptions of Italian styles of pizza draw extensively from "5 modi diversi di interpretare la pizza," Gabriele Valdès, www.agrodolce.it/2014/01/20/5-diversi-stili-di-pizza/.

[2] Enzo Coccia's terrific description of pizza gourmet, which ours is based on, can be found at www.enzococcia.com/pizza-gourmet-significato/.

[3] Our overview of American pizza styles is adapted from Liz Barett's *Pizza: A Slice of American History*.

Margherita Cones

Halal Pizza from Brunei

Pissaladiere

Puff Pastry Pizza

Sausage Pizza Bagel

Stuffed Crust Pizza

Italy's Best Pizza Maker

An Interview with Franco Pepe

Housed in a three-story, 17th century palazzo in the historic centre of the ancient town of Caiazzo, overlooking the Caserta countryside, Pepe in Grani is considered by many to be Italy's finest pizzeria. When proprietor Franco Pepe opened his doors in 2012 he was following in his father's and grandfather's footsteps, continuing a family business dating back to the 1930s.

But things have changed a great deal over the generations. Franco's grandfather was an agricultural labourer for a local farm who was paid by his employer in grain. Out of necessity, to support a family of six children, he started using the excess grain to bake bread for sale. He eventually became a full-time baker and taught his sons the trade, but as pizza became more and more popular in the mid-1900s the focus of the business shifted from away from breadmaking, with the family's first pizzeria opening in 1961. Franco was born a few years later and grew up in the apartment above the family pizzeria. He worked evenings with his father through school but after completing his ISEF studies went on to become a full-time teacher.

After his father's death in the mid-1990s, Franco and his brothers kept their father's pizzeria going for another 17 years before he made the fateful decision to leave his teaching post and return, full-time, to the family trade. But to commit himself fully he needed a fresh start.

"Once I made that decision the decision to leave teaching, I knew I had to leave the family pizzeria, challenge myself by starting something new," says Pepe. "If I stayed at the pizzeria, I would always be the son of Stefano Pepe. If I left, and put myself out there, I would be Franco Pepe."

When you decided to open Pepe in Grani there were people who doubted the wisdom of your thinking. What was your vision at the time?

Franco with family portrait (Giuseppe, Carolina, Francesco, Mario and Stefano Pepe; with Mario Fire [second from right]).

I'm not sure if you remember but in 2011 the Province of Caserta was caught up in the negative media coverage of the Terra dei fuochi and the mozzarella di bufala scandal. [1]

The people I knew in this province were honest people, they got up in the morning and did an honest day's work. I decided to bring these people around the table and say, "I want my pizza to serve everyone, to put the territory on my pizza." It was a real challenge at that time, to celebrate the bounty and excellence of a territory in the face of negative media coverage.

So that was the idea, and I wanted to bring it to life in the historic centre of Caiazzo, a small town of 5,000 people. I was enamoured with it because we lived there when I was very young and my grandfather's bakery was there. Though in reality the town was emptying out at that time. All the small businesses were suffering

from the influence of the large shopping centres that were opening up in the area. Many of them were closing.

It was a challenge even getting people to do the construction work in the historic centre because there weren't services. But I loved the place because of my family's history there, and I was fascinated by a certain 17th century palazzo located in a narrow little alley.

I thought, I'm going to open a pizzeria here, but something a little different. A place where, beyond the classical *sala* of the pizzeria, there would be a laboratory, and in addition to that an inn. A place where you could rest and experience something like slow pizza. A place where we could explore the possibility of creating a good, maybe even healthy, pizza.

It was a kind of invitation: come to my home, try my pizza, rest, and the next day I will take

Views of Pepe in Grani rooftop terrace overlooking surrounding countryside and dining room.

La Margherita Sbagliata with pomodoro riccio crudo.

you around the territory to see with your own eyes the places where our primary ingredients are made. To see the dairy where they make our mozzarella, the fields where our tomatoes are grown, the mill where our olive oil is pressed. So in 24 hours you get an appreciation, not just for my pizza, but of a true territory.

Today the historic centre of Caiazzo has been reborn, and artisanal businesses are reappearing. For example, in our alley there's a little bar that opens the same hours as we do. There's a parking lot that serves our customers.

We had a staff of seven when we began, and we'd make 150-200 pizzas per night. Now we have 33, and we make over 800 pizzas on a Saturday night. But we still try to maintain the craftsmanship and human know-how of our work, making everything by hand.

Tell us more about the idea of putting the territory on your pizza—the people you work with and the ingredients they produce.

The fragrance and flavour of the simple products of this region are truly exceptional, you have to experience it firsthand to really appreciate them.

When you talk about the producers, the *contadini* (farmers), it might convey an image of an old person going out to work in the fields. But today the young contadini are university graduates. They're returning to lands that were abandoned by their parents in favour of full-time office jobs. These young people are motivated and enthusiastic. They've gone back to the knowledge of their grandparents, who had a deep understanding of seeds and varieties. And they've built on this, with studies that analyze, evolve, and create markets for local products. It's serious research for the territory.

Through this kind work we've discovered forgotten varieties, like the *pomodoro riccio*, an exceptional tomato that dates back to the 1800s. It's very rich in polyphenols and antioxidants. That's where the idea for my *Margherita Sbagliata* came from. To really showcase the pomodoro riccio we don't bake it in the oven mixed with mozzarella and oil. We add it *al crudo* after the pizza is baked, so you get the true taste of the tomato.

That's just one example. Another is *creme di ceci* we also get from La Sbecciatrice, our pomodoro riccio producer. Or the *alife* onions we get from a young producer who has been cultivating them for us since about 2012—today her onions are widely available, even in the United States. Or our buffalo mozzarella producer from Il Casolare in Alvignano that is a family business that my grandfather worked with—our collaboration spans three generations.

There are many others, from Caserta and more generally from Campania: tomato varieties like *Piennolo del Vesuvio*, *San Marzano*, and an ancient variety that has been rediscovered in the area of Tramonti, a tomato that may be the grandfather of the *San Marzano* we know today, called *Re Fiascone*. It was probably the tomato that was used on the very first pizza Margherita ever made.

We can also talk about the national level, the made in Italy products. Today, for example, a group of the top cheese consortiums have entrusted me to showcase their products to the world, cheeses like *parmigiano reggiano*, *pecorino romano*, *caciocavallo silano*, and so on. I've created recipes for international events in places like Paris, Dubai, and Cologne. For me this signifies a validation of my work.

You're famous for making your dough by hand, a process you sometimes refer to as "wireless." What do you mean by that?

Photos starting top right: Chickpeas and pomodori riccci from Sbecciatrice; olive trees at Azienda Olivicola Petrazzuoli.

Monococco flour pizza, a collaboration with chef Fabbio Abbattista, the University of Brescia and Molino Piantoni.

When young people today learn the craft of pizza making, it's all about training to use machines. Everyone puts their faith in technology, which of course is useful for many things. But I ask you: when technology fails us, where is human know-how? Who knows how to make 800 pizzas a day by hand any more?

I talked about this recently when I was at the Las Vegas Expo, the largest pizza event in the world. We should teach young people how to make pizza without electricity—cutting the cheese with a knife, mixing the dough by hand, cooking with fire. Why? Because we can.

My method is very tactile and visual. What I want is to teach the younger generation how to make dough with their own hands, something that takes a lot of work and experimentation, but it's worthwhile. Otherwise this kind of knowledge will eventually disappear.

What can you tell us about "o Pepe," your own personal flour mix?

After 15 years of experimenting, I have developed my own blend of Italian grains that I use for my purposes only. But as you probably know, over the years grains don't remain exactly the same, so neither do flours. Therefore I'm always adjusting my own Pepe o blend.

In fact my philosophy is that there isn't a precise pizza recipe, because you're always adapting and modifying to account for atmospheric changes. For example, when I go to the United States, it's one thing to make dough in Los Angeles and another to make it in San Francisco. Yes they're both in California, but the water and the climate is different in each case. As artisanal pizza makers we adapt our recipe wherever we go, always modifying the blend to achieve a consistent result.

Stefano Pepe's favourite calzone: Cetera anchovies, Patelleria capers, Chiazzano olives and escarole riccia.

Is that one of the reasons you put such emphasis on research and experimentation in your work?

Yes. Today's grain is different than yesterday's. And it's the same with tomatoes or any other ingredient—they evolve over time. We have to continually evolve ourselves to maintain the quality and authenticity of our products.

As for my research, I'll give you a recent example: last week I presented a pizza at the Albereta in Frianciacorta. It was a wine pairing event, a collaborative project involving the young chef Fabbio Abbattista, the University of Brescia, the Molino Piantoni mill, and me. For the dough I experimented with a flour that Piantoni had made from 100% Monococco, an ancient variety that was one of the earliest grains used for baking—we're talking 10,000 years ago. I did not mix it with any other types of grain.

The Monococco has a simple gluten structure, and the team at the university found that it does not adversely affect people with gluten intolerances. So we were able to create a probiotic dough, a pizza that was not only delicious but healthy. That's not something a pizzaiolo could really say in the past.

I've read that the calzone on your menu is dedicated to your father, Stefano. What can you tell us about it?

It's not dedicated to my father—it was created by him! But the whole time he had his pizzeria, for over 30 years, it was never on this menu. It was something he made for himself.

One day, in 2003 or 2004, Professor Moio (University of Naples) came to see me and told me the great (food and wine critic) Luigi Ve-

117

Azienda Olivicola Petrazzuoli

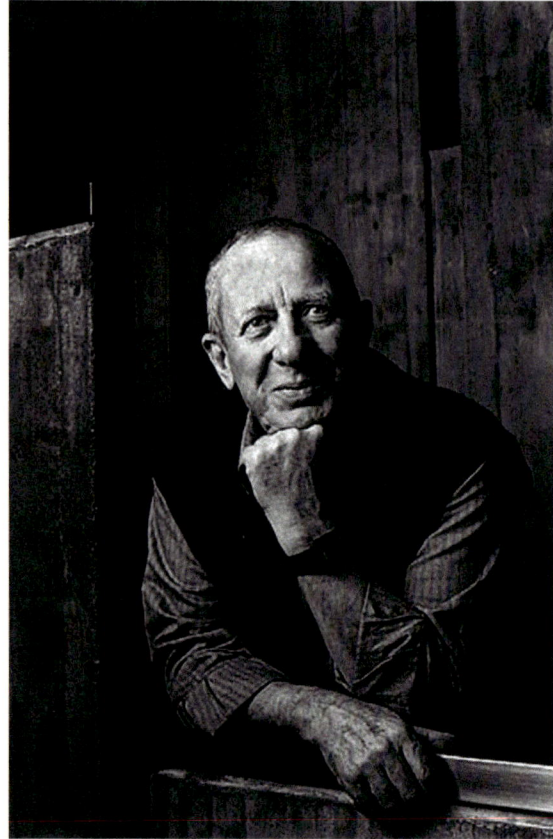

Luigi Veronelli

ronelli wanted to come and present one of his wines with one of my pizzas. But it had to be a pizza that paired well with the wine.

So I was thinking that evening, and I had this memory of my father, when I was young, sending me to buy the *escarole riccia* (curly escarole) and he would make his calzone with anchovies from Cetara, Pantelleria capers, Caiazzano olives, and a little oil. He didn't cook the escarole or add tomato or mozzarella, he just added it to the other ingredients, uncooked, and baked the calzone. And when it was baked he would have it with a glass of white wine.

I decided to make that recipe for Veronelli, who presented it with a Pallagrello Bianco Fontanavigna from Terre del Principe. That was the first time I really experienced the joy of Italian gastronomy and received media attention for my work, thanks to a three-page article written by Veronelli in his magazine.

Your family has seen many changes to the pizza industry over the years and no doubt things will continue to evolve. What are your predictions for the future of pizza?

I'd say there's two things I hope for—one is the collaboration between pizzaioli and experts from other professions. The other is the evolution of pizzaioli themselves.

Ask yourself, how many serious pizza schools are there in the world today? What pizza schools provide scientific training? Who knows how to make a healthy pizza? Today many pizza makers

Gambero Rosso pick for Italy's best Pizza Dolce 2018: Vesuvius apricots, lemon-infused buffalo ricotta, hazelnut & mint.

distinguish their flours by the colour of the bag rather than what's in it. And if you speak of polyphenols they don't know what you're talking about.

I've done many evenings with great chefs, and I've learned from those experiences, new and better ways for using primary ingredients. It's easy for us to collaborate because there's no confusion between the roles of the chef and the pizzaiolo.

That's an important distinction because pizza has always been, and will always be, a popular food. There's no such thing as a Michelin starred pizza—even if sometimes chefs and pizzaioli work together. Why do we sell 600-800 pizzas a day in a tiny town like Caiazzo? Because it's an affordable, accessible food, so anyone can eat it.

FOOTNOTE

[1] *Terra dei fuochi* (land of fires) refers to an area of Campania, primarily in the provinces of Caserta and Napoli, that were affected by an illegal dumping of toxic waste in the early 2000s.

Tools Of The Trade

OVENS

TRADITIONAL WOOD- AND COAL-BURNING OVENS

The earliest forms of pizza found in 18th century Naples were either fried or baked in large wood-burning brick and stone ovens. The design and popularity of these ovens evolved over the centuries, but until the post-World War Two era they were the standard pizza ovens found in Italy (primarily in Naples).

The earliest American pizzerias dating back to the early 1900s in Northeastern states like New York, New Haven, and New Jersey used coal instead of wood, simply because it was cheaper and easier to get at the time. This was the American standard until the invention of the portable, gas-fired deck oven in the 1940s—a development that paved the way for the quick rise in pizza's popularity in the second half of the 20th century.

The renaissance in artisanal pizza making that occurred across the globe since 2000 has rekindled interest in (and demand for) tradition ovens—especially traditional wood-burning Neapolitan ovens. And for the first time, advances in technology and design have made these ovens available on a global scale.

Neapolitan ovens are equally renowned for their high heat (over 500° C) and their aesthetic beauty—their exquisitely tiled exteriors and soft glowing flames make them a natural centrepiece for the modern upscale Napoletana-style pizzeria.

Many of these ovens are still fuelled with wood but there has also been a sharp increase in gas/wood hybrids and gas-only Neapolitan ovens. Gas is cleaner, easier to control, and a more consistent heat source than wood, and requires less expertise on the part of the pizzaiolo.

Another recent innovation is the rotating baking surface, which evenly cooks the pizza with-

Fire, gas, and electric ovens at the Faema Canada showroom. Photo: Rick O'Brien.

out the need for manual turning by a skilled master pizza maker—a tricky and time-consuming task that can be challenging during peak times at a busy pizzeria.

GAS AND ELECTRIC DECK OVENS

When the New York firm Baker's Pride invented the factory-built, gas-fueled oven in the 1940s it was a game changer for the pizza business. Simply put, the spread of pizza chains and "slice shops" that started in the US in the 1950s and spread around the globe soon afterwards could not have

occurred without the invention of the deck oven.

Suddenly the cost of manufacturing, installing, maintaining, and fueling a pizza oven dropped dramatically. Production capacity spiked, because deck ovens were space-efficient and stackable. Even the dough changed, as new recipes had to compensate for lower temperatures and longer baking times than pizzas made in traditional coal and fire ovens.

Historically, the majority of deck ovens were fueled by gas because it was cheaper and more powerful than electricity. But the standard seems to be shifting as electric ovens become more powerful (now capable of temperatures over 800° C) and sophisticated in terms of functionality.

Unlike gas, electric deck ovens have top and bottom heat sources so you can customize according to the style of pizza: pan pizza is cooked primarily from below, for example, whereas a pizza slice reheated directly on the hearth of the oven might be the exact opposite. Top-of-the-line electric ovens even offer the option of front/back heat differentiation for further customization, such as when heat loss needs to be offset from a frequently opened oven door.

Modern electric ovens are also highly programmable—daily on, off, and self-cleaning

Bottom left: Moretti conveyor oven at Faema. Top left: Neapolitan oven with rotating cooking plane from Italiana FoodTech. Top right: Gas deck ovens at Pizza Nova. Gas deck ovens at Pizza Nova. Photos: Rick O'Brien

times can be pre-programmed. And they're much easier to install because they don't require a gas line or ventilation.

CONVEYOR OVENS

The more customized ovens become, the less skill required of its operator. This of course reduces labour costs and makes personnel losses less risky for business owners.

The best example of this in terms of pizza ovens is the commercial conveyor oven, invented in the 1970s. As the name suggests, the uncooked product is simply placed on a conveyor belt at one end of the oven and collected, fully cooked, on the other. Conveyor ovens come in a wide variety of sizes and can even be stacked depending on the needs of the pizzeria.

DOUGH MIXERS

From large commercial kitchens to small artisanal ones, the vast majority of pizzerias use a dough mixer of some kind. There are a variety of styles but in each case the objective is essentially the same—to gently, evenly mix and knead the dough without heating it up or "stressing" it from overworking.

Two of the most effective styles of mixer for making pizza dough are the spiral and twin arm. In contrast to planetary mixers (like those used in home kitchens) these mixers feature a rotating bowl, which in the case of a spiral mixer slowly spins countercurrent to the spiral arm.

The twin arm mixer—considered by many top pizzaioli as the most effective—was designed to simulate the motion of two human arms mixing and kneading the dough. Its slow, methodical "diving" arms perfectly oxygenate the dough, resulting in a lighter, airier product.

Moretti electric ovens from Faema Canada with refractory stone cooking plane & top and bottom heat sources.
Photos: Rick O'Brien

123

Rounders, dividers and spreaders at Italiana FoodTech. Photos Rick O'Brien

ROUNDERS, DIVIDERS, AND SPREADERS

Not quite as ubiquitous as dough mixers, these machines are nonetheless quite common in commercial kitchens, especially large scale and high volume ones. They're also a good fit for non-specialists, such as full-menu restaurants that offer pizza on the menu but don't have the depth of expertise you'd expect at an artisanal pizzeria. The benefits are easy to understand:

• Speed: automatic machines that cut and form up to 800 balls of dough and flatten up to 400 pizzas per hour
• Precision: consistency of size, weight, and width that's virtually impossible to achieve by human means
• Cost-savings: automatic and semiautomatic machines are a fraction of the cost of a full kitchen

Some stretchers even have customizable settings that mimic the movement of human hands to give the finished product a more rustic, natural, "handmade" feel.

Mixers, rounders and dividers at Faema Canada.

Baking Pan and Pan Grippers; Photo: Rick O'Brien

BAKING PANS

Baking pans come in a wide variety of shapes and sizes—the right one for your needs depends on the finished product you want to produce.

Coupe-style aluminum pans are great for New York-style pizza; deep dish pans are suitable for Chicago style; Italian ferro blu (blue iron) give you the crispy bottom and hydrated dough that's best for pizza in teglia. Perforated and meshed pans, and pans with "nibs" (small bumps) are also quite common, which improve airflow for a crispier exterior, and also to prevent moisture buildup causing sogginess after baking.

Thickness, colour, and finish are also considerations. Darker pans tend to absorb heat while lighter ones reflect it. Thicker pans take longer to heat up, slowing down the cooking process and resulting in chewier cooked pizza. Uncoated pans require periodic seasoning while silicone glazed pans do not.

This page: Italian blue iron pan and gripper and pizza dough proofing boxes from Italiana FoodTech. Photos: Rick O'Brien

OTHER TOOLS AND ACCESSORIES

Scrapers and dough cutters: standard tools for manually handling and dividing the dough.

Digital Scales: traditional pizza recipes and most professional bakers measure their ingredients by weight, so a digital scale is essential in

Firewood at Queen Margherita Pizza. Photo: Rick O'Brien

Morning bread at Pizzeria Libretto. Photo: Rick O'Brien

the pizza maker's kitchen.

Dough boxes: designed to keep dough hydrated and cool while it ferments, traditional dough boxes were made of wood, while today's space-efficient, dishwasher-friendly models are made from synthetic materials like polypropylen, Teflon, and fibreglass.

Firewood: For safety and performance the best types of wood to use for a fire-fueled oven are hardwoods such as oak, maple, ash, beech, and birch. Optimal size for the individual pieces of wood is 3 inches in diameter and 12-18 inches long. Water content should be 15-20%.

Peels: used to place the raw pizza on the hearth of the oven and remove it when cooked. Perforated peels allow excess flour to fall off the pizza before it goes into the oven, reducing the risk of burning and leaving a slightly bitter taste.

Spinners: Traditional Neapolitan ovens have a single heat source, so the pizzaiolo must carefully rotate the pizza with a spinner to get a uniformly baked pizza.

Oven tools at Queen Margherita Pizza. Photo: Rick O'Brien

Infrared thermometer at Itaiana FoodTech. Photo: Rick O'Brien

Brushes, ash shovels, and ash guards: tools for keeping ash from the burning wood off the hearth of the oven where the pizza is baked. Brushes are typically made with brass bristles that won't damage the refractory stone.

Hook: used to move logs and stoke the fire.

Oven doors: the door of a wood oven is used to help retain heat when the oven is not in use. This reduces the time needed to reheat the oven the following day. Some traditional Neapolitan pizzerias bake bread first thing in the morning, while the oven is still hot, before the oven is turned on.

Infrared thermometer: shines a laser onto any spot inside a fire-burning oven to read its temperature.

Pan gripper: for pan pizza makers of all kinds, from pizza al teglio to Chicago deep dish.

Pizza cutters (or rotella taglia pizza)

Copper canisters: for adding olive oil to the pizza before or after cooking, AVPN guidelines call for the use of *un orciuolo in rame con becco sottile*, a copper canister with a long narrow spout typically used in traditional pizzerias. These receptacles are prized for their fine, consistent, tidy pour (no dripping or spillage), and the way they keep the oil slightly cool in temperature. And of course they convey a certain nostalgia you just don't get with a squeezable plastic condiment bottle.

Insulated pizza bags: invented by Ingrid Kosar in Chicago in 1984, these bags have become a standard tool in the pizza delivery business. About a decade later the American firm Check Corporation upped the game with the invention of the electrically heated pizza bag.

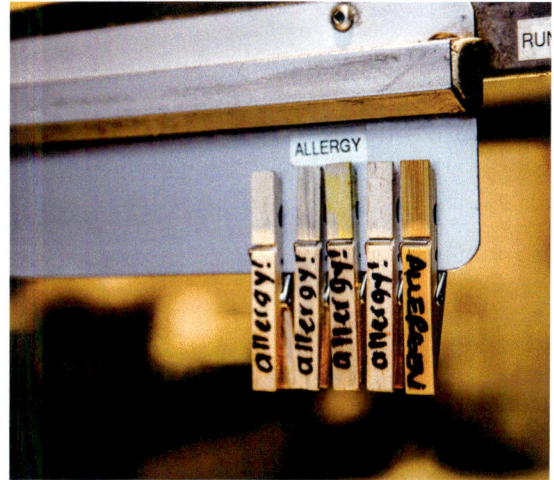

Dietary needs tracking at Pizzeria LIbretto.

Copper canister at Viva Napoli.

Rechargeable electric-heated pizza delivery bag.
Photo: Rick O'Brien

Master Oven Maker Stefano Ferrara

A Third Generation Craftsman

Stefano Ferrara is amongst the most revered wood oven makers in the world. Growing up in Naples, he learned his craft from his father and grandfather, and today he is passing that knowledge on to his 25-year-old son, the fourth generation of an 80-year-old family business. "He still needs a bit of experience," says Stefano with a smile, "but he's following in our footsteps."

Stefano is deeply committed to the tradition of making artisanal, hand-made ovens. But at the same time his products and his business have evolved significantly over the past two decades, as the popularity of Neapolitan pizza continues to grow across the globe.

Today his ovens can be found in the United States, Canada, France, Germany, the UK, Japan, Australia, Korea, and beyond.

Tell us about the origins of your business.

In the early years my grandfather made a kind of community oven that you saw around Naples in those days. A family would visit once a week and make bread and other baked goods, whatever they needed for the week. When my father learned the trade, he started making ovens for pizzerias as well. Eventually that became our focus.

From the time I was very young I was always attracted to this kind of work. After school I would go work with my father because I wanted to learn the trade. I really enjoyed it. I was 10 years old when I started. Today the business has changed a great deal but we still make our ovens exactly the way my father did—brick by brick, handmade.

Can you describe the process for building one of your traditional "fixed" wood-burning ovens?

First, the raw materials are shipped to the location from our facility in Naples, and we go there in person to build the oven. It takes a week to construct, and three people to do the job.

It's a very particular, manual process. Every step—making the cement, hand-cutting the tuff stone, laying the bricks—has to follow its own sequence and timeline that must be respected. So in total it takes a week. Then you need another seven to ten days for the oven to dry. Or more accurately for it to dehydrate—in the sense that it must dry very slowly to ensure a good result.

Is it true that this type of oven takes a long time to heat up when it's first used?

Yes. Or if it hasn't been used for some time. The reason is because of the humidity that builds up inside of the oven and slows down the heating process.

On the other hand when an oven is being used daily, and the pizzaiolo covers the opening when he's finished for the evening, it's still around 230-240° C the following morning. In fact many pizzaioli make bread with the oven

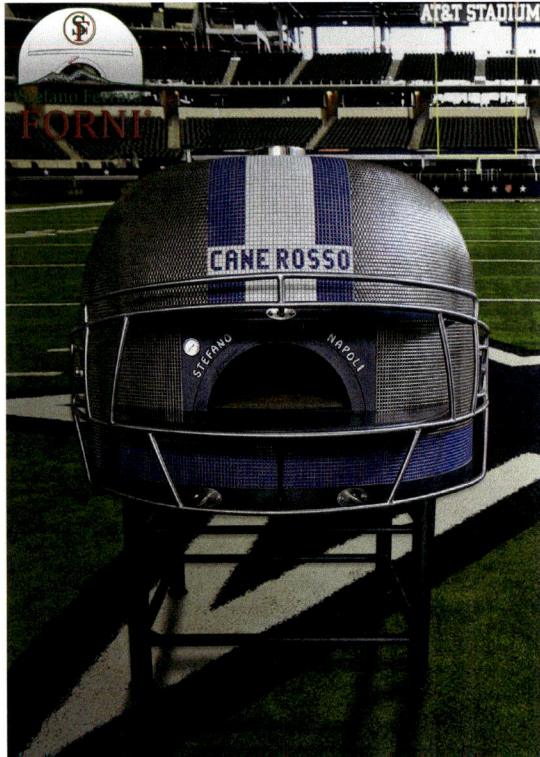

Oven for Cane Rosso in Houston, designed to look like football helmet. Photo: Stefano Ferrara Forni

still off before they reheat it to 400-450° C for making the pizzas.

The primary materials you use, like Biscotto di Sorrento and Pietro di Tufo, are from the Naples area. What can you tell us about their characteristics and why you use them?

The cooking plain (floor of the oven), on which the dough is baked directly, is made of Biscotto di Sorrento. It's made by our artisans using volcanic clay, pressed by hand, the way it's always been done. When you do it by hand rather than a mechanical press, you get tiny microcosms of air—invisible to the eye—that retain the heat when cooking.

Pietro di Tufo is a type of rock that is typical of this region, that's cut in large blocks from the hills. Tuff stone is a natural insulator—it absorbs heat and releases it very slowly. In fact in our area

grapes are grown in these hills because of its heat absorbent qualities of the stone. Many buildings here in Naples are made from tuff stone as well. The Spaniards for example built everything with it.

When you compare archive photos to today's ovens, the aesthetic today is more sophisticated. What can you tell us about this aspect of the business?

It's more of a modern thing, a part of the business of pizza that has spread all over the world. Every client wants to find that perfect oven that will make their pizzeria the most beautiful. It gives me a great deal of pleasure—I really enjoy the challenge of helping clients realize their vision.

We do all of the design ourselves. My daughter, who works with me, draws the original concept by hand, then my workers bring it to life, one piece at a time, using ceramic tiles or Pal-

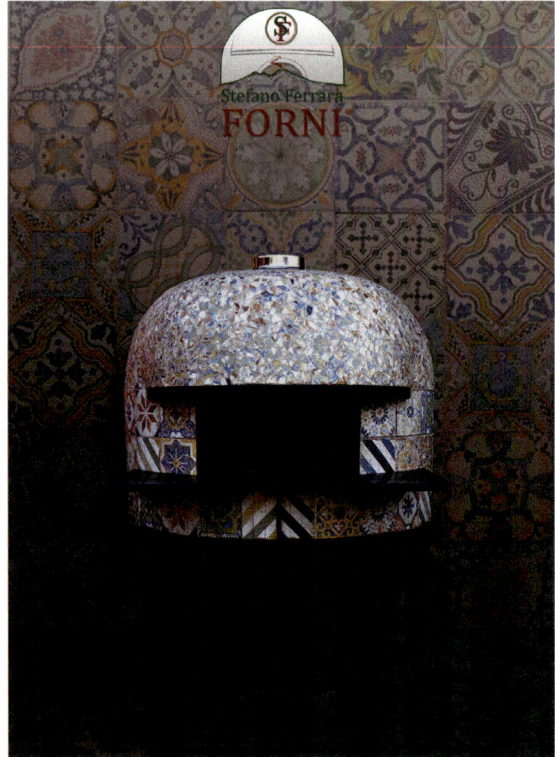

Top left and right: Piatto (Moncton) oven design and oven. Photo: Stefano Ferrara Forni

ladiana marble for the exterior. It's all done by hand, nothing is prefabricated.

Today you make mobile ovens as well as fixed ones. When did you start making them?

About 20 years ago, I had this idea of making the traditional oven, brick-by-brick as we've always made it, but mounted on a mobile structure. I did this because of the changing needs of our clients, many of whom were far away from here. Obviously they don't all have the means to bring in an artisan from Naples to construct a fixed oven. With a mobile oven the client is still getting something made in the traditional way, but they save money.

You have also branched out into gas and electric ovens. What's the secret for protecting the quality of your products as you evolve?

Maintaining the just equilibrium—of the cooking plain, the vault, of the dimensions of the oven. If you respect this equilibrium the oven will perform beautifully. But if some measure or proportion is off, the oven won't work properly.

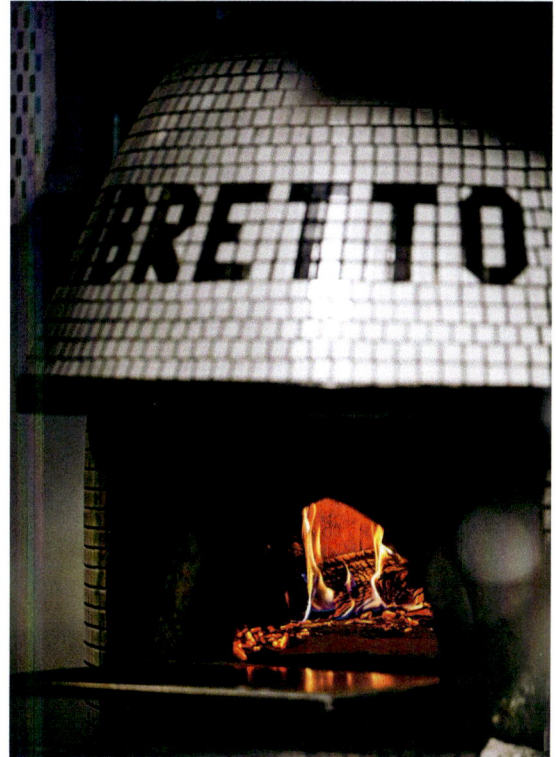

Toronto's first Stefano Ferrara oven. Photo: Stefano Ferrara Forni

The other important thing is the construction of oven below the cooking plain. But that's a secret, as they say, that I keep to myself.

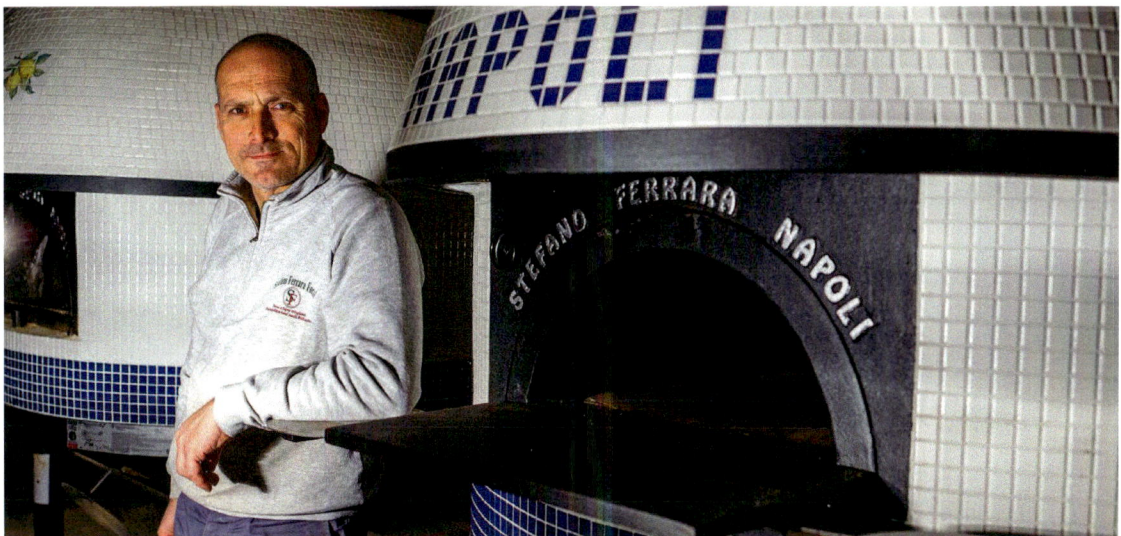

Stefano Ferrara. Photo: Stefano Ferrara Forni

Ingredients and Toppings

FLOUR

The vast majority of pizza makers around the world today use various types of white flour made from soft wheat. Hard wheat—which produces a coarser, amber-coloured powder known as semolina—is more commonly used to make pasta.

THE GRAIN OF WHEAT

The grain of the wheat plant is made up of three parts:

• *The bran:* the outer layer that protects the kernel and contains fiber, antioxidants, iron, and vitamins.

• *The germ:* the seed or embryo of the plant, containing vitamin B, healthy fats, and other nutrients.

• *The endosperm:* the primary source for white flour, high in starch and proteins.

The milling process for white flour sifts and refines the grain until the endosperm and germ are removed, leaving a fine white powder that is high in protein and sugar and low in fats and nutrients, which gives it a long shelf life and high elasticity.

FLOUR STRENGTH

A critical factor in a flour's performance is its protein content, which regulates gluten levels. Gluten is what gives the dough elasticity when it is properly kneaded or leavened.

When bakers talk about the "strength" (or the W count) of a flour, they are referring to its protein level.

Flour, yeast, and sea salt. Photo: Rick O'Brien

- Weak flours, with protein levels of 7-10%, are ideal for pastries, cakes, and cookies.

- Medium flours, with 11-12% protein, are commonly used for pizza, focaccia, or a non-crumbly sweet like banana loaf.

- Strong flours, with 13-16% protein, are traditionally used for bread making.

Products that need a longer leavening period and higher water content require a stronger flour, which is why the recent trend towards longer proofing periods in pizza making has resulted in pizza makers using stronger doughs. Gabrielle Bonci, for example, recommends American home cooks use bread flour (12-14% protein) to make his pan-style pizza, since the type of flour he typically uses is only available in Italy.

In fact the high hydration capacity of bread flour makes is ideally suited for homemade pizza, because lower temperatures and longer baking times can dry out the dough.

TYPES OF FLOUR

Milling processes and flour classifications differ between Italy and North America, which often causes confusion for pizza makers.

In Italy, soft wheat flour is categorized according to the fineness of the grain—00 being the most refined, integrale (whole grain) the most coarse. Generally speaking, the coarser the grind the higher the protein level of the flour, but there are other factors that influence the strength of the flour; for example, blending a weaker wheat variety with a stronger one.

Interest in traditional Italian pizza has spiked both within Italy and around the world over the past few decades, and a constant topic of conversation amongst professional and home chefs alike is whether 00 flour is the best flour for pizza. The correct answer to this question is, "kind of..."

Yes 00 is the most common flour used by pizzaioli in Italy, revered in particular for the lightness of the dough it makes. But in practice, most Italian pizzerie use blends of flours to increase things like digestibility and nutritional value (which is lost when wheat is highly refined). Pizzaioli are constantly experimenting with their personal blends in search of the elusive perfect pizza dough.

Luckily for novices just learning the craft, and larger commercial enterprises that require a greater degree of standardization, big Italian mills like Caputo and Cinque Stagioni have developed many pre-made blends specifically created for the different styles of pizza: Pizza "00" Napoletana, Pizza Tradizionale, Pizza Teglia, and so on. Perfect for pizza makers who haven't quite reached Tre Spicchi status just yet.

ALTERNATIVE FLOURS

Whole grain flours are much higher in nutrients than refined flours, especially when they are ground slowly (or stone-ground), the best way to preserve the natural properties of the grain. But they're also harder to work with and have a stronger taste than refined flours. For this reason, recipes for whole grain pizza typically blend lighter flours like 0 or 00 with whole grain flour.

With the rising interest in healthier and gluten-free products, as well as heritage plant varieties and biodiversity, there are also a number of non-wheat grains now available in Italy and North America.

In Italy, kamut, farro, and spelt are historic grains that have gained traction in both pasta and pizza making in recent years, on account of their flavour profile and nutritional value. In the

Bread flour close-up

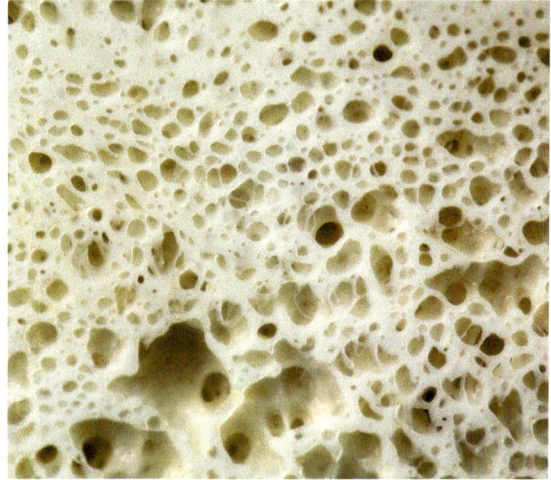

Cake flour close-up

Cake flour pizza

Bread flour pizza

Cake, All-purpose, Double Zero and Bread flours

This flour strength demonstration created by Chef Luciano Schipano shows effects of different protein levels in soft wheat flours. The airiness and elasticity of the bread flour dough (top right) starkly contrasts the density of the cake flour dough (top left) after each has been cold-proofed for an eight-hour period. The bread flour produced a pizza that was light and crispy (middle right), whereas the cake flour pizza was heavy and dense, essentially inedible (middle left).

Photos: Rick O'Brien

Kamut flour pizza at Pizzeria Defina. Photo: Rick O'Brien

US, gluten-free flours like brown rice, millet, and quinoa are becoming increasingly popular.

YEAST

Yeasts are leavening agents that give pizza and bread doughs their characteristic lightness. They are single-cell organisms that consume the natural sugars in the flour, converting them to carbon dioxide, which causes the dough to expand.

There are a variety of yeasts used in pizza making today: natural or sourdough starters, and commercial ones like fresh, dry active, and instant yeast.

NATURAL YEAST (LIEVITO NATURALE O MADRE)

Until the commercial production of yeast start-ed in the 19th century, natural starters were the only way a baker could leaven dough. They require more time and skill than commercial yeasts, but they are also healthier, more digest-ible, and longer lasting, which is why they are still commonly used today.

Natural yeast can be created from scratch by combining flour and water and exposing the mixture to naturally occurring bacteria in the air until it begins to ferment, then feeding the mixture with additional wheat and water on a re-current basis for several days. Once mature, the yeast can be kept alive indefinitely if it is stored and fed properly.

The other form of natural levitation is to al-ways put aside a piece of dough for future use—sometimes called mother yeast or a sourdough starter. The starter is reactivated by adding water and flour and can also be kept alive indefinitely.

FRESH AND ACTIVE DRY YEAST

Fresh yeast is the standard leavening agent used by pizzerias in Italy, but it's not all that common here in Canada and the US. It's sometimes called "cake yeast" because it's sold in bars, or brewer's yeast (lievito di birra) because it was originally extracted from beer barrels. Fresh yeast is simple to work with because it does not need to be rehydrated. But it's also less stable, harder to maintain, and does not last as long as dried yeast, which is why large scale North American kitchens tend to avoid it. Home cooks looking for fresh yeast can find it at traditional grocers and bakeries.

Active dry yeast is essentially dehydrated fresh yeast (technically they are both saccharomyces cerevisiae). Its strength is more consistent than fresh yeast, which is why it's more widely used, even though it requires the extra step of re-activating the yeast (proofing it, by adding water) prior to making the dough.

INSTANT OR RAPID-RISE YEAST

Invented in the 1970s, instant yeast is a finer and more potent powder than dry active yeast, and does not require proofing. It's simply added to the dry ingredients before they are mixed with water. For ease of use it has become the standard in North American kitchens.

TOMATOES

As discussed in chapters 2 and 3, the tomato is not a native Italian plant. It was brought from America in the 16th century as a decorative plant, and was generally considered inedible until the 18th century, when street vendors in Naples started using it as a condiment for pasta. Pretty soon after the practice was adopted by

Lievito di birra (brewer's yeast). Photo: Rick O'Brien

the city's pizzaioli, who till this point had always made their pizzas bianca.

To this day the San Marzano DOP tomato, a sweet, fleshy variety with relatively few seeds, is considered the gold standard pizza condiment. Many chefs like Pizza Libretto's Rocco Agostino swear by it: "I've done a lot testing with different tomatoes and this one is my favourite," he says. "It's the simple nuances of the tomato: the sweetness, the acidity, the texture. It's the rich volcanic soil and the air in the area of Mount Vesuvio."

Other varieties from the region like Vesuviano and Corbarino are equally valued but much harder to find outside of the Campania region.

RAW OR COOKED?

Traditional Italian pizza is made with raw tomato, but when American pizza chains and frozen pizza manufacturers sprang up after World War Two they opted for cooked tomato sauce instead. Cooked sauce is a more scalable commercial product: it lasts longer and its taste profile is easier to standardize compared with raw products.

Pizza made with cooked, seasoned tomato sauce is still pervasive in North America, but most artisanal pizzerias these days use raw tomatoes.

PELATI, POLPO OR PASSATA?

Italian pizzerias generally use skinned whole tomatoes (pomodori pelati) but in Italian home cooking polpa (pulp) and passata (skinned, de-seeded, tomato puree) are sometimes used instead.

Skinned tomatoes are the most flexible product: they are crushed manually or lightly pulsed in a food processor to attain the desired coarseness. (Immersion blending is discouraged because it infuses air into the sauce, and if there are some seeds still remaining they will be combined with the sauce, giving it a slight bitterness and orange tinge.)

Polpo is essentially a convenience product—you get the coarseness of crushed, skinned tomatoes right out of the package. Passata is similarly convenient but creamier in texture and generally higher in water content. Both these products are suitable substitutes for skinned tomatoes and can be used interchangeably depending on your taste.

Queen Margherita Pizza. Photo: Rick O'Brien

CHEESE

The story of cheese on pizza is a bit like that of tomatoes: traditional Italian mozzarella is a fresh product made from water buffalo milk, meant to be eaten within a day or two after it's made. But during the post-World War Two era a more durable, low-moisture, semi-hard mozzarella made from cow's milk was created for use in the rapidly expanding fast- and processed-food industries. This is still the standard pizza cheese used in most countries outside of Italy today.

It's worth remembering however that pizza in its original form—the kind that was sold on the streets of Naples in the 18th and 19th centuries—was often made without cheese (or even tomato). Simply put, cheese (especially fresh cheese) was an expensive ingredient for the urban lazzaroni who ate pizza on a daily basis.

In fact, even the three pizzas that Raffaele Esposito famously made for Queen Margherita of Savoy in 1889 only included one that was made with mozzarella. The second was topped with fish and the third with lard and caciocavallo, a semi-hard cheese that was more commonly used on pizza at the time, because it was less expensive and kept longer than fresh mozzarella.

HOW MOZZARELLA IS MADE

The term mozzarella comes from the verb mozzare, meaning "to cut," a reference to the traditional cheese maker's task of separating a small piece of pasta filata and forming it into a ball of cheese. The process of making mozzarella is surprisingly simple:

1. Milk is combined with rennet, citric acid, and warm water to form curds.
2. The curds are gently cooked for a short time and then separated from the whey.

Rennet added to heated milk to form curds.

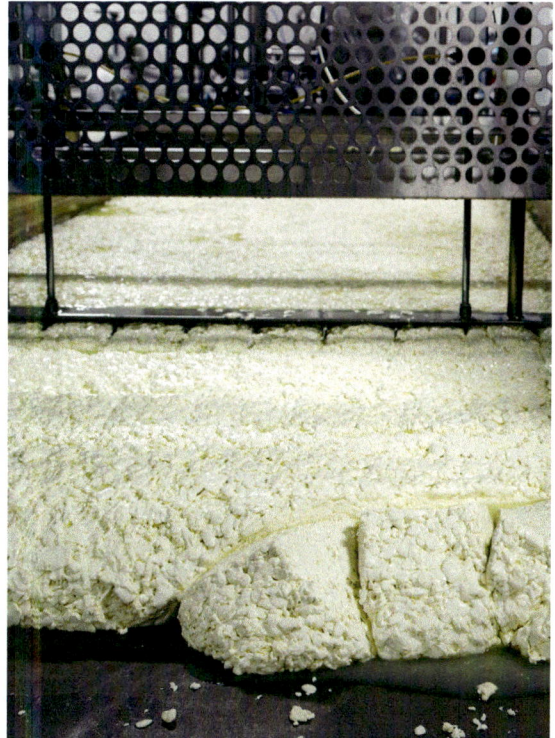
Curds separating from the whey.

Curds heated, kneaded, extruded as pasta filter.

Pasta filata formed into 6 oz balls and cooled.

Production at Quality Cheese. Photos: Rick O'Brien

Distributor Tony "Cheese" Cohan has introduced authentic Italian cheese to many local restaurants and pizzerias Photo: Rick O'Brien

3. The curds are re-heated and kneaded to form the stringy consistency of a pasta filata.

4. The pliant mass of cheese is then cut into small pieces of 20-80 grams and formed in balls, then placed in cold water to harden.

Today balls of mozzarella and fior di latte are usually formed by die-cast machines to ensure consistency of size and weight, while more labour-intensive shapes like nodini ("knots") and treccie (braids) are still crafted by hand.

MOZZARELLA DI BUFALA AND FIOR DI LATTE

The pizza margherita that Esposito named after the Queen of Savoy was made with mozzarella di bufala, the only kind of mozzarella available at the time. Today the cheese is made throughout Italy and many places around the world, although production of EU-certified mozzarella di bufala DOP is restricted to certain areas of Campania and Lazio.

Mozzarella di bufala is famous for it's soft texture, creamy flavour, and porcelain-white hue. Compared with cow's milk fior di latte it is higher in calcium, protein, and fat, but lower in cholesterol.

Because cow's milk has a higher water content than buffalo milk, fior di latte is lighter in taste and fat content. It's also more durable than buffalo milk, one of the factors that makes fior di latte cheaper to produce, and therefore more scalable as a product.

Fior di latte is the denser of the two cheeses so it's often cut thinner (2-3mm versus 5-6mm for mozzarella di bufala). Both cheeses need to be drained of excess water for about half an hour after they are cut to avoid pooling of water and sogginess on the cooked pizza.

PEPPERONI

Pepperoni is North America's most popular pizza topping, made from cured, minced beef and pork, and seasoned with paprika and chili peppers. There are various theories on the exact origin of pepperoni, but one thing's for sure: it did not come from Italy.

The earliest written records of pepperoni date back to early the 20th century when Italian butchers—mostly from Southern Italy—started to flourish in New York City. The name "pepperoni" probably derives from peperoncino, the

Italian word for hot peppers, which are often used to give southern Italian varieties of salami their characteristic heat. This type of salami is itself used on classic Italian pizzas like alla diavola and is the closest thing you'll find to pepperoni in Italy.

Since the year 2000 a number of higher-end American salami makers—people like Paul Bertoli of Fra' Mani in Oakland and chef Dan Drohan of Otto in Greenwich Village—have been attempting to reinvent pepperoni as an artisanal product. They've gained limited traction at iconic pizzerias like Bianco in Phoenix and Delfina in San Francisco.

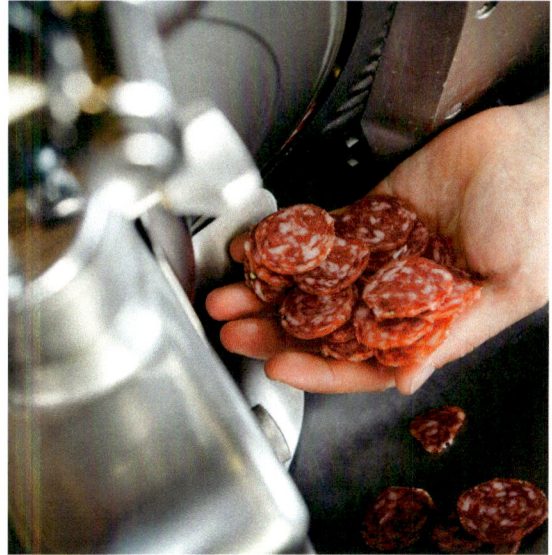

Fresh-sliced artisanal pepperoni. Photo. Rick O'Brien.

CLASSIC ITALIAN TOPPINGS

MARGHERITA
Tomato, mozzarella di bufala (or fior di latte), and basil.

The emblem of Italian pizza and still its most popular version, regardless of region or style of crust (neapolitan, romana, etc).

The Dr. Pepperoni at Maker Pizza. Photo: Rick O'Brien.

Napoletana/Romana Il Gatto Nero. Photo: Rick O'Brien

Capricciosa, Terroni. Photo: Rick O'Brien

MARINARA
Tomato, garlic, oregano.

This so-called seafarer's pizza is Margherita's less famous (but older) cousin, especially outside of Italy. Marinara is the other variety of TSG pizza, meaning it's officially recognized and protected by the European Union. Its simplicity harkens back to a time when pizzaioli had to improvise with the sparse ingredients at their disposal, a time when cheese (especially fresh cheese) was not always available. And yet out of scarcity an enduring classic was created: the marina is as popular as ever in Italy, especially in the city of Naples.

NAPOLETANA OR ROMANA
Tomato, anchovy, oregano; (optional) capers.

Strange—and confusing for non-Italians—yet true: the same pizza that is called napoletana in most of Italy is called romana in the city of Naples itself. Adding to the possible confusion is that neither term refers to the romana or Napoletana style of crust in this context. In any case if you order a Napoletana in Rome or a romana in Naples, this is what you get.

CAPRICCIOSA
Prosciutto cotto, artichoke, (white button) mushrooms, pitted olives, mozzarella, tomato; sometimes boiled egg, anchovies (preserved in olive oil).

The Italian equivalent of "the works," this famous pizza is called "capricious" (witty, unpredictable) because it has something for everyone. This includes (at least) one too many ingredients by classical standards, which gives it a playful feel. Tip: don't use artichokes marinated in herbs—it offsets the balance of flavours on the pizza.

QUATTRO STAGIONI
Prosciutto cotto, artichoke, (white button) mushrooms, pitted olives, mozzarella, tomato.

The Four Seasons is a deconstructed Capricciosa: instead of mixing the ingredients together the pizza is divided into four sections, each featuring a different topping that represents a different season: artichoke for spring, olives for summer, etc.

Quattro Stagioni, Terroni. Photo: Rick O'Brien

Quattro formaggi pizza at Via Mercanti. Photo: Rick O'Brien

QUATTRO FORMAGGI

Four cheeses, varying from place to place, with or without tomato.

The "four cheese" pizza is typically topped with a mix of strong and mild cheeses, often (but not always) containing gorgonzola. Other cheeses commonly used are mozzarella, scamorza, provolone, fontina, emmental, gruyère, grana padano, parmigiano reggiano, and pecorino romano. The key to a great quattro formaggi pizza is balance, good quality ingredients, and knowing how different cheeses react in the oven.

DIAVOLA

Tomato, mozzarella, spicy salame, pecorino cheese; (sometimes) black olives

Viva Napoli's Diavolona, a variation on the Diavola. Photo: Rick O'Brien

Pizza ortolana at Viva Napoli. Photo: Rick O'Brien

Pizza Primavera at Via Mercanti. Photo: Rick O'Brien

Italian's say alla diavola (of the devil) for different types of spicy dishes such as pizza, pasta, and meat dishes. Pizza alla diavola is made with slices of spicy salame (like soppressata) and grated pecorino cheese for extra bite. Unlike prosciutto cotto which is always added after the pizza is cooked, the spicy sausage in the recipe is cooked on the pizza like North American pepperoni.

FUNGHI OR PROSCIUTTO E FUNGHI
Tomato, mushroom; sometimes with prosciutto cotto and/or cheese.

These are standards you'll find on any pizzeria menu across Italy. There are many variations on the classic pizza ai funghi—with or without sauce and cheese, types of mushrooms, and so on.

ORTOLANA
Mozzarella, sweet peppers, eggplant, zucchini; (sometimes) tomato, seasonal vegetables.

Ortolana means "from the garden"—a healthy blend of roasted seasonal vegetables served on pizza or pasta. As a pizza it is served with or without tomato. Although zucchini, eggplant, and peppers are a standard combination, many other vegetables can be used (like asparagus, broccoli, cherry tomato) according to season and locale.

PIZZA PRIMAVERA
Mozzarella, cherry tomato, arugula, prosciutto crudo, grana padano shavings.

To make a "spring" pizza, the raw cherry tomato, arugula leaves, prosciutto crudo, and hard cheese shavings are added to a freshly baked pizza bianca topped with mozzarella or fior di latte. Tip: tear the arugula leaves as you add them to the pizza to bring out their latent aroma and add flavour to the pizza.

FRUTTI DI MARE
A mix of local seafood, garlic, parsley.

Pizza comes from Naples, an ancient port city, so it's no surprise that seafood has been served on pizza for hundreds of years. Today seafood pizza is popular all over Italy, more so than in North America. Typically the seafood is sautéed separately and added to the pizza, fully or at least nearly cooked, depending on the recipe. Generally

The Capo Faro at Pizzeria Defina, a variation on frutti di mare. Photo: Rick O'Brien

speaking Italians don't mix seafood and fish with cheese, so this pizza is normally served without.

MARE E MONTI

Pomodoro, funghi, gamberetti and/or cozze and calamari, aglio, prezzemolo; (sometimes) mozzarella.

The Italian peninsula is famous for its mountains and its seas, both represented on this classic pizza. When a pasta or pizza is prepared "mare e monti" it combines seafood and vegetables—mushroom and tomato are most commonly used on pizza mare e monti but variations exist. And yes, occasionally mozzarella is added, despite the general bias against cheese combined with seafood.

PUGLIESE

Tomato, mozzarella, red onions.

Puglia is well known for its focaccia barese and calzoni, but just as famous in Italy is this simple pizza made with tomato, mozzarella, and finely sliced red onion—a classic combination you'll find at any traditional pizzeria. Occasionally black olives and/or capers are added.

CAPRESE

Fresh tomato, buffalo mozzarella, basil; (sometimes) oregano.

A relatively recent invention that's gaining in popularity in Italy, this salad-on-a-pizza reflects a growing trend towards crudo (raw) ingredients on pizza, popularized by people like Gabrielle Bonci. The cheese and tomato are sliced thin and added while the pizza is hot, so they are very gently "cooked," just enough to adhere to the dough.

147

Wild Mushroom pizza at Defina, a variation of pizza funghi. Photo: Rick O'Brien

BOSCAIOLA
Mozzarella, button mushrooms, sausage.

This so-called lumberjack pizza is topped with mozzarella (or fior di latte), mushroom, and pork sausage, a classic combination of condiments as popular with pasta as they are on pizza. The boscaiola can be served with or without tomato according to your preference.

CANADIAN VARIATIONS

HAWAIIAN

Whether you see it as a claim to fame or source of infamy, so-called Hawaiian pizza wasn't actually invented in Hawaii but right here in Ontario. Chatham, Ontario to be specific. That's where Greek-born restaurateur Sam Panopoulos and his brothers ran the Satellite Restaurant, which offered American and Chinese-American style dishes. The story goes that Panopoulos' exposure to sweet and savoury flavour combinations in Chinese cooking gave him the idea of topping a pizza with canned pineapple and Canadian bacon.

Hawaiian pizza has always elicited strong reactions, both for and against. In early 2017 the debate went unexpectedly viral when Icelandic president Guðni Th. Jóhannesson made the off-the-cuff remark that the dish should be banned. The international storm that ensued in social and mainstream media forced the president to temper his original statement, showing the indelible mark Chatham has left on the global pizza market.

Hawaiian Pizza, Pizza Nova. Photo: Rick O'Brien

2013 Pizza Expo Champion 'Nduja Pizza, Defina. Photo: Rick O'Brien

Donair Pide, Defina. Photo: Rick O'Brien

Duck Confit, Libretto. Photo: Rick O'Brien

Recipes

HOMEMADE PIZZA (PIZZA CASARECCIA)

Recipe by Toronto-based chef / consultant Luciano Schipano
(originally from the town of Olivadi in Catanzaro, Calabria).

Most of us don't have professional grade pizza ovens capable reaching 900 degrees at home, so it's difficult to replicate many of the pizzas featured in this book.

This recipe by chef Luciano Schipano however is a classic pan pizza found in diverse regions all over Italy, especially in the South. It's also a very common antipasto served at family gatherings in Italian diaspora communities in Canada and the US.

The recipe will vary from region to region and even between neighbors in the same town (each of whom will claim to be the most authentic!). And of course ovens, pans, room temperatures and humidity levels all have their effects—a little trial and error is usually needed to find the right balance for your taste and your kitchen.

Some people will add a pinch of sugar to the dough, to help caramelize (i.e. brown) the crust during baking. Others will add olive oil to boost its crispiness and hydration. It all depends on your desired results.

The same goes for toppings—Luciano likes traditional Calabrian ingredients like 'nduja, dried black olives and oregano. Growing up in Italy it was common to top your pizza with whatever was in season or stocked in your cantina (soppressata, pancetta, mushrooms, onions, etc).

INGREDIENTS FOR THE DOUGH

- 400 grams all-purpose or bread flour
- 240 grams lukewarm tap water
- 8 grams fine sea salt
- 1 gram fresh yeast
- (Optional) 20 grams extra virgin olive oil

TOPPINGS

- 500 ml crushed or puréed Roma or San Marzano tomatoes, seasoned with 20 grams extra virgin olive oil and a pinch of salt. Add water if it is too thick.

- 400 grams shredded scamorza
- 0 grams 'nduja
- QB black olives
- QB dried oregano
- QB salt to flavour tomatoes

INSTRUCTIONS

1. Dissolve the yeast in warm water.

2. Add the flour to large mixing bowl and carve out a hollow space in the middle to pour in the water.

3. Pour in the water, a little at a time, constantly mixing. Once all the water has been added add the salt and (if you are using it) olive oil.

4. Continue on mixing till the ingredients are fully combined and start to form a soft dough.

5. At this point the dough becomes a little less sticky and you can start to knead it by hand. Continue kneading for 10-15 minutes until it's fully integrated (there is no more dried flour or bits of dough stuck to the side of the bowl).

6. Gently transfer the dough to a well-floured hard surface and continue to kneading by hand for another 5-10 minutes, till the dough is smooth and slightly firm.

7. Place the dough in a lightly oil a large bowl (at least twice the size of the dough), cover with a heavy cloth or plastic wrap, and place in the refrigerator overnight (10-12 hours). (If you press your finger into the dough and it bounces back into shape, it's ready for proofing).

Photos: Rick O'Brien

8. Preheat the oven to 450°

9. Remove the bowl from the refrigerator about 90 minutes before baking, so it can come to room temperature before you put it in the oven.

10. After an hour, empty the dough into a lightly oiled pan, approximately 30 x 40 cm, and spread it out evenly with your fingertips

11. Evenly spread puréed tomato over the entire surface of the pizza, leaving just ½ inch space from the crust

12. Sprinkle on a layer of cheese, a scattering of black olives, and the 'nduja. The 'nduja should be applied in small dollops, about a third of a teaspoon each. Let the pizza sit, all dressed, for 5 minutes or so before baking.

13. Bake on the lower rack of the oven for 20-25 minutes, until the bottom of the crust is slightly browned.

14. Remove from the oven and let rest for 5 minutes before cutting. Serve hot or at room temperature as a nice addition to the antipasto table at your next party.

Photos: Rick O'Brien

153

FOCACCIA BARESE

By Toronto-based chef & culinary tour guide
Massimo Bruno (originally from Bitritto, Puglia).

This is one of my favourite snacks and a staple antipasto at my kitchen studio events. It's also a very popular street food from my home province of Bari: as kids we'd always stop for a slice at the local bakery on our way home from school.

Focaccia barese can be made with or without olives—I like both but I usually make it with-out because not everyone likes olives. I usually make it with cherry or pachino-style tomatoes but plum tomatoes are great too, as long as they are fresh and in season.

I recommend fresh yeast for this recipe. It's not as common here in Canada as in Italy but quite often you can find it at your local bakery.

INGREDIENTS

- 325 grams bread flour
- 50 gr semolina
- 200 ml tap water (cool, not cold)
- 1/3 cup extra virgin olive oil
- 1 half-pound potato, boiled
- 1/2 ounce fresh yeast or 1/2 pack dry active yeast
- 20 gr fine sea salt, plus more for sprinkling
- 1 tsp sugar
- Oregano QB

Photos: Rick O'Brien

YOU'LL NEED

A 12 or 14 inch round or 9 x 12 inch rectangular pyrex pan

INSTRUCTIONS

1. In a small glass, dissolve the sea salt in ¼ cup warm water.

2. Prepare your yeast according to the instructions on the package.

3. In a mixing bowl, add remaining warm water and olive oil. Slowly mix in the flour and semolina, the yeast, crushed potato, and finally the dissolved salt.

4. Keep working the dough till it becomes smooth but still a bit wet and sticky, approximately 5 minutes.

5. Coat the bottom of the pan with olive oil and pour the dough into it. Lightly oil your hands as well to prevent sticking.

6. Flatten the dough towards the edges of the pan. Cover with plastic wrap and set aside for 90 minutes in a warm place. (I use the oven with the light on, but make sure it's not on if you do this!).

7. Preheat oven to 425°.

8. Uncover the pan. Break the tomatoes into small pieces by hand over the focaccia, letting the juices run onto the dough. Lightly press the pieces into the dough (rather than just placing them on top).

9. Sprinkle the focaccia with oregano and drizzle generously with olive oil. Then finish with a healthy sprinkle of sea salt.

10. Bake for 20-30 minutes depending on the strength of your oven. Keep a close eye the first time you make it to avoid burning—you want the focaccia to be golden brown on top and bottom.

ADDITIONAL NOTES

The dough can be made 1-2 days in advance and kept refrigerated. Keep it in a plastic bag but not fully sealed. Don't forget to let it come to room temperature before baking!

CECINA TOSCANA

By olive and wine producer Gaia Massai (originally from Prato, just outside of Florence, Tuscany). Reprinted from gaiasplate.com.

Cecina is the Tuscan version of chickpea flatbread, an easy and ancient recipe that goes back to the Etruscans, who were big consumers of chickpeas. Given its high energetic power, it was born as a breakfast but among farmers was often eaten in the fields for lunch, accompanied by pecorino cheese, prosciutto, and a glass of Chianti.

Cecina is still very popular along the Tuscan coast, especially in Livorno where even today you can ask for a "five and five," meaning five cents' worth of bread and five cents' worth of cecina.

PREPARATION TIME: 10 MIN
COOKING TIME: 20 MIN

Serves 4-6

- 180g (1½ cup) chickpea flour
- 3 tbs of extra virgin olive oil, plus some for greasing the pan
- 2 sage leaves and one half rosemary sprig (optional but highly recommended)
- salt and pepper QB
- 2 cups of water

Photos: Rick O'Brien

INSTRUCTIONS:

1.   Preheat the oven to 500° F. Grease a 26cm ovenproof dish with extra virgin olive oil.

2.   Put olive oil in a small bowl with the sage leaves and rosemary sprig, and let it rest for at least 30 minutes.

3.   Pour water into a large bowl and gradually add the chickpea flour, stirring constantly. Stir in the olive oil after removing the sage and rosemary and add one tsp of salt and a generous pinch of black pepper.

4.   Pour the batter into the greased pan—the batter should not be more than 1cm (1/2 inch) deep.

5.   Bake for 20 min and broil for 3-4 minutes until the top is golden yellow and cracked.

6.   Transfer to a serving plate and sprinkle it with pepper. Serve hot with pecorino cheese and salami, accompanied by a glass of Chianti.

Photos: Rick O'Brien

FOCACCIA DI RECCO

By Tuscany-based food writer and
photographer Emiko Davies. Reprinted from food52.com.

The people of Liguria, a region along Italy's western Riviera, know a thing or two about how to produce a decent focaccia. The region's best known iteration, focaccia Genovese, is fluffy in the middle with a crisp crust doused in olive oil and salt flakes. It's a favourite for breakfast (dipped into cappuccino) or as a snack (often washed down with a glass of local white wine).

But Ligurian focaccia doesn't stop at one type, as towns all over Liguria produce their own focaccia. The town of Recco, known as Liguria's gastronomic capital, produces one that is a revered delicacy—so much so that in 2012 it received IGP (protected geographical indication) status by the EU. So technically, just as Champagne is only from Champagne, you can only get Focaccia di Recco in Recco.

This focaccia is rather simple: a paper-thin crust sandwiching oozy fresh cheese. As legend has it, when the citizens of Recco were in hiding during the Crusades, they created this focaccia with what little they had (flour, water, olive oil, and some cheese). Today you can find it in every bakery, pizzeria, and restaurant in town.

Like many regional specialties, the rules behind how the focaccia di Recco is produced are strictly traditional. It can be round or rectangular, but the important thing is the dough must be as thin as possible. It must be pulled and stretched by hand until you can read the newspaper through the other side. Bread flour gives the dough great elasticity, which means it's easier to stretch the dough without breaking it. You can do it with all-purpose flour, but you may need to handle it more delicately. Once the dough is less than one millimeter thick, it is

Photos: Emiko Davies

placed on a baking sheet or pizza tray and dotted with creamy, super fresh cheese.

The cheese is important. It should be good quality, very fresh Crescenza or stracchino cheese. The "official" website of the focaccia di Recco uses double the amount of cheese I do, so feel free to get cheesy on this one.

Then, another thin layer of dough is placed on top and little holes are cut to let steam escape. That top layer is brushed with olive oil and sprinkled with salt before hitting the oven until crisp and golden and the cheese has melted. It's a pure joy to eat.

This recipe makes 3 to 4 focaccias.

INGREDIENTS

- 3 cups (400g) bread flour
- 3/4 cup (200 milliliters) water
- 1/2 cup (100 milliliters) olive oil, plus more for greasing and drizzling
- 2 teaspoons (10 grams) salt, plus more for sprinkling
- 1 pound (500g) stracchino or Crescenza cheese

INSTRUCTIONS:

1. Using a wooden spoon, mix the water, olive oil, salt, and 1 cup of flour in a medium bowl until smooth. Add the remaining 2 cups of flour little by little, mixing with the spoon until thoroughly combined. Knead by hand in the bowl for 5 minutes or until smooth and elastic (poke it; it should bounce back easily). Let rest, wrapped in plastic, in the fridge for 2-3 hours.
2. Preheat the oven to 480° F (250° C), and grease a baking sheet or a round pizza tray with olive oil.
3. Divide the dough into 4 even pieces and

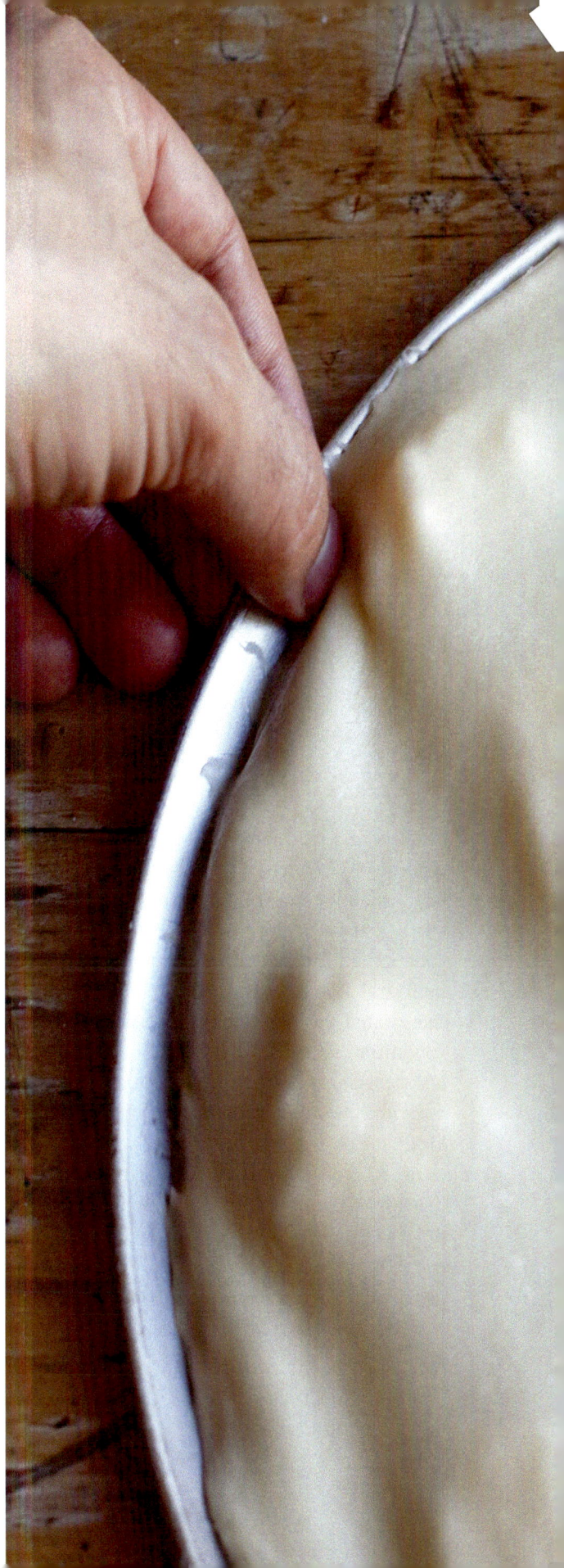

keep them under a tea towel or wrapped in plastic wrap when not in use. Roll out the dough ball initially with a rolling pin on a floured work surface, then begin stretching it carefully with your hands, using the weight of the dough to help stretch it. Get the dough as thin as you can, then transfer it to the prepared baking tray. Lay spoonfuls of the cheese over the dough. Take another piece of dough and roll and stretch again as before. Lay this layer over the cheese. With a knife, a rolling pin, or your hands, tap the edges of the dough together all along the border of the tray to trim the dough to exactly the size of the tray (see pictures for reference). Go over the edges of the focaccia again with your thumb, pressing down to seal the edges of the two layers of dough. Gather the excess dough, and roll into a ball to use for the next focaccia.

4. Pinch the top of the dough in 5 or 6 places to create holes for steam to escape. Drizzle the top of the focaccia with a bit of oil and sprinkle with a pinch of salt. Bake for 7 minutes, until lightly golden brown and the cheese has melted.

5. While the first focaccia is in the oven, prepare the second with the remaining dough (adding the scraps from the first to the balls of dough) and bake when the first is out of the oven. I recommend only baking one at a time as the distribution of heat will be compromised with more than one in the oven.

6. The dough can also be frozen (wrap it tightly in two layers of plastic wrap and then freeze). Before using the dough, defrost overnight in the fridge or for a few hours on the counter. The dough will keep in the freezer for up to 3 months.

TORTA AL TESTO

By New York-based chef, writer, and culinary tour guide
Michelle Capobianco. Reprinted from majellahomecooking.com.

Torta al testo is a traditional flatbread sandwich from Umbria stuffed with vegetables, cheeses, and cured meats. The torta is cooked on a heavy testo, a circular iron griddle placed directly on the stovetop (long ago, the disc was made from clay and placed over coals in the fireplace).

When I was a student in Perugia with about 10,000 Lira per day to spend on food (about $5 US back in the pre-Euro days), I regularly frequented a hole-in-the-wall Forno on a narrow cobblestone street near the university that specialized in this savoury regional specialty. Each day after classes, I ordered a torta al testo for lunch and brought it up to Corso Vanucci, the wide pedestrian-only promenade in the centro storico that was ideal for people-watching. My favourite filling for these fluffy, oiled flatbreads was peppery arugula, sweet pacchino tomatoes, and creamy stracchino cheese.

Last summer, during a mini-break from Abruzzo, we visited Umbria, and I returned to Perugia for the first time since 1997. I dragged my husband and three sons around the maze of backstreets behind the university for nearly half an hour in search of my beloved Forno. I resigned myself to the fact that I wouldn't find my old haunt, picked up some pizza al taglio for my hungry kids, and set off for Gubbio where we were staying for a few days. The next day, as we were exploring the lovely medieval town, I asked a local shopkeeper from whom I purchased a testo (called a panaro in Gubbio) where we could enjoy a good torta al testo (which, incidentally, is called crescia in Gubbio) for lunch. They sent us to Osteria dei Re, a charming osteria and wine bar with al fresco dining in a picturesque piazza, where we were treated to the torta al testo of my memories.

Here's an easy recipe that you can prepare in

Photos: Michelle Capobianco

your favourite well-seasoned cast iron skillet. Prepare the dough in the morning and enjoy them for lunch or refrigerate the dough overnight and simply bring it to room temperature prior to griddling the flatbreads. The uncooked dough stays very well—how do I know this? Because I was in the process of making the flatbreads for a play-date luncheon when my five-year-old broke his collarbone. The remainder of the dough went in the fridge and I prepared it the following day with his favorite filling of fresh mozzarella and tomatoes).

Once griddled, the flatbreads should be enjoyed very soon after you prepare them, as they tend to become stale rather quickly. If you need to wait, wrap them tightly in plastic after they cool off and reheat in a whole oven prior to serving and filling.

This recipe serves 4 people.

INGREDIENTS

- 1 tsp active dry yeast
- 3 cups all-purpose flour
- 1 tsp sea salt
- 2-3 tbsp extra-virgin olive oil, plus more for drizzling

IDEAS FOR FILLINGS

1. Stracchino or taleggio cheese and baby arugula
2. Sauteed greens (spinach, chicory, chard, broccoli rabe, etc.) with grilled or pan-fried sausage
3. Tomatoes, fresh mozzarella, and basil
4. Grilled vegetables
5. Italian oil-packed tuna and sun-dried tomatoes
6. Speck and fontina
7. Prosciutto and shaved Parmigiano or mozzarella di bufala
8. Mortadella

Photo:

9. Nutella and bananas (find me something with which Nutella doesn't pair well!)

INSTRUCTIONS

1. In a small bowl, stir together yeast and ½ cup of hot water. Let it sit until foamy, about 10 minutes.
2. Combine flour and salt in a food processor and pulse to combine. Stir 1 tablespoon of olive oil into the activated yeast mixture and with the food processor running, pour it in.
3. Process until a dough forms (i.e. when the ingredients no longer adhere to the sides of the bowl). If the dough is too dry, add some cool water, one tablespoon at a time until this happens.
4. Transfer the dough to a lightly floured surface and knead for about 5 minutes.
5. Form the dough into a ball and transfer to a large oiled bowl. Cover the bowl tightly with plastic wrap and allow the dough to rise for about 1½ hours in a warm place.

6. Punch the dough down (the dough should have doubled in size) and divide it into two balls. Lightly flour one piece of dough, and using a rolling pin, roll it into a 9" disc.
7. Place the disc on a floured baking sheet, poke it all around with a fork (this will prevent too many air bubbles during cooking), and repeat with the remaining dough.
8. Heat one tablespoon of olive oil in a 10-12" cast-iron skillet over medium heat. Working in 2 batches, cook each dough disc, flipping occasionally, until light brown on each side, about 8-10 minutes total.
9. Lay one of the flatbreads on a cutting board, add your desired filling, place the other flatbread on top, and with a serrated knife, cut the torta into 8 wedges. Drizzle with a little more oil and serve.

Buon appetito!

Pizza Goes To College

When you step into The Local Restaurant in the Centennial College Culinary Arts Building, one of the first things you notice is the pizza oven, front and centre of the view into the restaurant's open concept kitchen.

The Local is part restaurant, part training facility for culinary arts students at the college. The oven's prominence in its physical space (and on its menu) signifies the importance of pizza making in Centennial's culinary program.

It's also a reflection of the restaurant industry as a whole: pizza was an ethnic snack food when it first appeared in Ontario in the 1950s; today it's arguably the city's most popular dish.

American-style takeout slices and delivery pizza; Italian-style eat-in pizzerias; bakeries; Italian

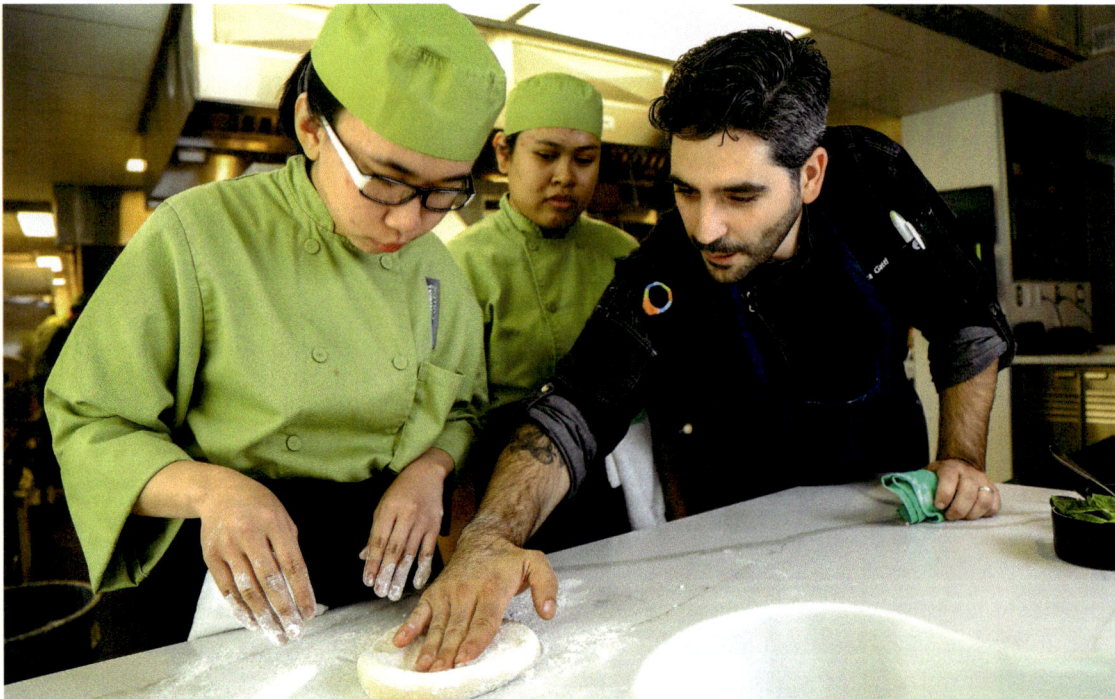

Luca Gatti with students at The Local Restaurant. Photo: Victor Virgilio

and non-Italian restaurants; pubs; even grocery stores, where prepared foods are becoming increasingly common—the list of places where fresh-baked pizza is made keeps growing year after year.

"We have a pizza oven that's central in our restaurant, even though this is not an Italian restaurant, because it's such a part of the DNA of the restaurant scene in Canada," says Joe Baker, dean of Centennial's School of Hospitality, Tourism and Culinary Arts.

"The whole point of this facility is to get people ready to work in the industry. And since pizza's such a staple in the culinary world, we make it a part of every student's experience," says Baker.

Baker adds that the versatility of pizza allows the restaurant to incorporate it into its lunch, dinner, and brunch menus, in each case taking a slightly different approach. It's also what makes pizza the perfect platform to showcase local, seasonal ingredients grown by the students themselves or sourced from producers in the area.

"We don't really stick to traditional menu items," says Baker. "We stick to core fundamentals. That's what gives you the ability to be creative based on what's available."

The Local's head chef Luca Gatti, whose resume includes stints with some Toronto's top pizzerias and eateries, wants to instill a passion for pizza in his students by teaching them the craft of making it from scratch.

"We want to encourage students to think of it as an important part of our menu, not a fast food," says Gatti. So he teaches fundamentals of artisanal pizza making: forming a proper dough ball; long fermentation times of up to 3 days; hand stretching (not rolling) the dough; and so on.

"We try to make students understand how the longer proofing of the dough changes the taste and blistering of the finished product," he says. He characterizes the pizza at The Local as

Joe Baker. Photo: Victor Virgilio

somewhere between Neapolitan and traditional Italian, but adds that the real goal is to teach students the essential skills of pizza making rather than mastering any specific style.

"There are restaurants and pizzerias opening left, right, and centre in the city," he says, "they're looking for young people who can grow with the company and learn the way their pizzaiolo does things."

He uses the example of his own experience working with Pizzeria Libretto (Neapolitan pizza) and Descendant Pizza (Detroit style). "They're so different from each other," he says, "it's a completely different thought process. If you're too focused on one way of doing things you'll never be able to learn new approaches. I try to teach students that this is how we do it here but there are plenty of different styles. And they're all great."

Photo: Victor Virgilio

Tips For Wine And Pizza Pairing

The pairing of pizza and wine is hardly an ancient art. Unlike pasta—Italy's other famous dish—it's only in the past few decades that Italian food and wine critics (and pizzeria owners) have started to think seriously about it.

During this time it's become apparent that unlike North Americans, who often default to reds, Italians favour whites, rosés and sparkling wines with their pizza.

What's their advice for the perfect abbinamento della pizza? Here are a few tips to get you started.

PAIR THE WINE WITH THE TOPPINGS

At the risk of stating the obvious, choosing the right wine for your pizza depends on the condiments. A frutti di mare (seafood), a caprese (cherry tomato, arugula, prosciutto) and a diavola (spicy salame, pecorino cheese, tomato) are very different pizzas and the choice of wine to accompany them should reflect this.

KEEP IT LIGHT AND LIVELY

Tannic, full-bodied, wood-barrel aged reds are great for pairing with red meats, aged cheeses and heavy pasta sauces. But when paired with pizza they often overwhelm. Young, light, crisp wines that clean the palate between bites (rather than lingering on it) are ideal.

COMPLEMENT AND CONTRAST

A fruity, sparkling, semi-sweet Lambrusco is the perfect foil for a savoury salame or sausage pizza. A bubbly and aromatic Oltrepò Pavese Moscato nicely cuts the sharpness of the gorgonzola on a quattro formaggi. The right contrasts add a dimension to your meal.

WHITES WORK WELL, STILL OR SPARKLING

Simone Padoan has famously said that champagne is the perfect accompaniment for pizza, but for those on a budget prosecco or cava will do just fine. Greco di Tufo, Verdicchio, and Chardonnay are amongst the most popular whites enjoyed with pizza.

IF YOU ONLY DRINK REDS...

There's no rule against reds with pizza, but younger, medium bodied, aged in stainless steel often work best. Pinot Noirs, Chiantis, Vino

Rocco Agostino pairs his signature spicy 'nduja pizza with an effervescent Lambrusco. Photo: Rick O'Brien

Nobile di Montepulciano, and Gamays are safe bets in most cases. Even a bolder, more tannic wine like Primitivo can work in the right places (with pizzas with red onions or hot chilis for example).

AND FINALLY… THE CASE FOR GRAGNANO

Special consideration must go to Gragnano, a red frizzante produced in the region of the same name, just east of Naples. When Neapolitans drink wine with pizza, this their go-to.

Importer Robert Tomé (Stem Wine Group) says this blend of Aglianico ("the Barolo of the south") with Piedirosso and Sciascinoso (both of soft tannin structure, plum, cherry and blueberry nuances) produces a "chameleon" of a wine that seems to adapt to any food its paired with.

"A couple of years ago I was visiting Iovine Winery in Gragnano, and was treated to a lunch that lasted the full afternoon," he says. "We started out with some different pizzas: a Margherita, a fiery Vesuvio (hot salsiccia and peppers), then a white pizza with greens and potatoes. Next was pasta e fagioli, followed by whole grilled orata, then a sorbetto."

After a little break and passeggiata, the meal unexpectedly recommenced: a grigliata mista of sausage, lamb and beef was served on a massive platter was served with fresh green salad… to help the digestion."

When the feast was finally over Tomé asked his host, Aniello Iovine, why the same wine was served with so many different dishes, he replied, "Because I wanted to show that Gragnano is one of the most versatile wines on the planet!"

And that's why it pairs so well with the many styles and varieties of pizza.

167

Domenic Meffe

and

Romi's Pizzeria & Ristorante

By Rita Simonetta

Domenic Meffe is a man who has achieved great success in the hotel industry as the founder and owner of Monte Carlo Inns™, but you might be surprised to discover that he credits pizza with providing the foundation for his business accomplishments. That's because before delving into the hotel industry Meffe ran a thriving restaurant, Romi's Pizzeria & Ristorante, where pizza was the main attraction.

"Pizza gave me so much; it was the beginning of my success," he explains. "It's a wonderful food that's tasty and easy to make. Plus, it can be customized with different ingredients that produce diverse flavours. My favourite pizza is well-done with a thin crust and lots of olive oil, sliced tomatoes, bocconcini and anchovies."

In 1966, a year after emigrating from Campobasso, Molise, the then-15-year-old immediately got a job at a Toronto pizzeria where he learned everything from making pizza dough to expediting deliveries.

The owner, Pasquale, served as a mentor. "He was always so pleasant to his clientele," recalls Meffe. "I learned work ethic and how to treat customers."

And that's something Meffe integrated into his own business practices as head of Monte Carlo Inns™, which comprises eight hotels in the Greater Toronto Area. Fittingly, the restaurant menus at Monte Carlo Inns™ include pizza.

"It's so popular," Meffe explains. "There's nothing better than seeing a group of people enjoying a pizza," says Meffe, adding that it's the ultimate sharing food. "And you can eat it anywhere—in your backyard, in the park or on a work site."

In 1973, Meffe took over Romi's Pizzeria & Ristorante at 3062 Bloor Street West. The restaurant, which he sold in 1985 before switching over to the hotel industry, is now owned and run by his sister and brother-in-law.

Romi's continues to be a success thanks in part to its solid beginnings. "We made quality food, and we treated customers with care," says Meffe.

Domenic Meffe

Photo: D.Meffe

Photo: D.Meffe

Meffe ran the restaurant with the help of his wife and together they created homemade fare like BBQ chicken, spaghetti, lasagna, steak sandwiches, and of course, pizza.

"The most popular pizza was a small size pepperoni," Meffe recalls. "That was the seed of our success."

The hard-working businessman, who has a wood-burning oven from Italy in his backyard, still finds time to make pies at home for his family. "The best slice is one you can hold up," he says. "It's an art."

And whether he was making pizzas at the beginning of his career or cooking them nowadays for pleasure, Meffe always dedicates himself to the challenge ahead.

"You have to be passionate about everything you do in life," he says. "I put my whole heart in whatever I take on."

Photo: D.Meffe

ONTARIO'S BEST FOR QUALITY AND VALUE.

SEE WHY WE TRULY ARE
YOUR HOME AWAY FROM HOME.

Whether it's for business or pleasure, choose the hotel more people trust across Southern Ontario. Featuring impressive luxury suites with whirlpools and our exclusive signature "sleeping on a cloud" mattresses, Monte Carlo Inns will give you a level of comfort that is simply beyond compare.

Locations throughout Southern Ontario
1-800-363-6400 | montecarloinns.com

CONNECT WITH US

Monte Carlo Inn

Monte Carlo Inns
Your Home Away From Home™

IT'S ALL ABOUT *the Basics*

"Dough, Sauce and Cheese. That is the foundation of a great tasting pizza."

– Domenic Primucci

PIZZA NOVA®

SINCE 1963

WE RAISE REAL NEAPOLITAN PIZZA

Pizza Napoletana Le 5 Stagioni: flour just as they want it in Naples.

Pizza Napoletana flour was created in partnership with Associazione Verace Pizza Napoletana, the authentic Neapolitan pizza association, in accordance with suitability specifications set out by these masters of pizza making. Its superior quality and special elasticity has made it the most sought after and best loved flour both in Italy and abroad.

Since 1831

le 5 Stagioni

LA PASSIONE PER LA PIZZA

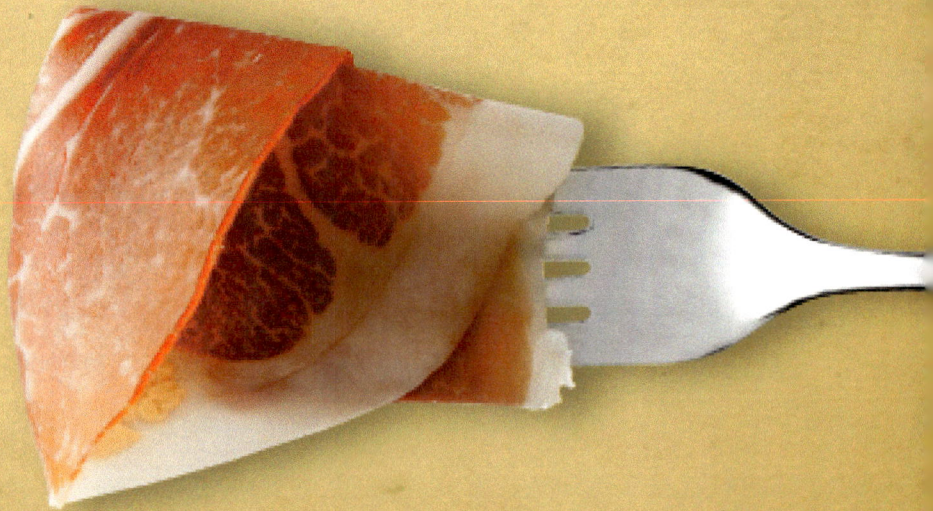

STELVIO

NORTHERN ITALIAN RESTAURANT

354 QUEEN ST. W TORONTO

www.stelviotoronto.ca

+1 416.205.1001

PIZZA
IS ALWAYS THE
ANSWER.

Photo by John Liviero

ACCORDO
DI FILIERA
DEL GRANO DA MACINA
CONSORZIO AGRARIO
DI LATINA
CAMPO CAPUTO

Neapolitan Gold.

Still and only from wheat.

Few people know that a good wheat mixture gives life to a magic harmony between the flour and the pizza maker, bearer of this neapolitan tradition. Obtaining the smallest, perfect flour granule requires a lot of work.

We select our wheat with the utmost care, stock by stock, following specific tests, and we handle it with an innovative procedure.

The secret is there, you can't see it, but you can taste it from the very first bite.

CAPUTO
1924
Il mulino di Napoli

JAN K. OVERWEEL
LIMITED / LIMITÉE

186

Imported by Jan K. Overweel Limited | www.jkoverweel.com | Contact: sales@jkoverweel.com

www.molinocaputo.it   Join us on f

JUST BECAUSE IT LOOKS ITALIAN DOESN'T MEAN IT'S ITALIAN

Look for the real thing. Authentic Italian products crafted in Italy.

Made in Italy

italianmade.com

Pizzeria VIA MERCANTI
2010

🍕 Dine In   🎉 Special Events

🍽 Catering   🔥 Take Out

👑 Private Functions

Locations

188 Augusta Ave,
Toronto, M5T 2L6
(647) 343-6647

1501 Gerrard St East,
Toronto M4L 2A4
(647) 352-2206

87 Elm St,
Toronto M5G 1X8
(416) 901-1899

163 Buttermill Ave,
Concord L4K 3X8
(905) 669-8100

...RELLA BASIL GARLIC

...PESTO $11

...ANZANE BUFFALO RICOTTA 11

...E MOSTARDA AGLIATA 12

12

12

★

**FULL MENU
AVAILABLE
FOR TAKEOUT**

★

★ APERITIVO 4-7 ★

OUR BAKERY

CORNETTO CON NUTELLA
DI PESCA
CANNOLI SICILIANI
BISCOTTI CON MARMELLAT...
DI CAFFE E NOCC...

AMARETTI SICILIANI
TORTA CIOCCOLATINO
PIZZELLE
BABA NAPOLETANO
BOMBOLONE
ASSAGGI DI PASTICCERIA
MINI FRITTATA O SCHIACCIATA
CAFFÈ COMPLETO

**Monday to Friday: 7:30am - 2:00am
Saturday & Sunday: 8:00am - 2:00am
Brunch Saturday & Sunday: 10:00am - 4:00pm
Daily Aperitivo: 4:00pm - 7:00pm**

bar
BUCA

Buca.ca 📷 @BarBuca

QUEEN
—
MARGHERITA
—
PIZZA

Taste is Objective, Quality is FACT

Toronto's Best Prix Fixe
Open Noon Until Close at Leslieville, Baby Point & Dundas West Locations

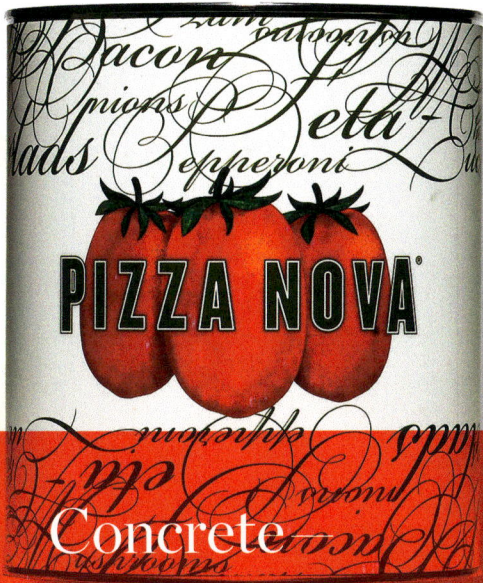

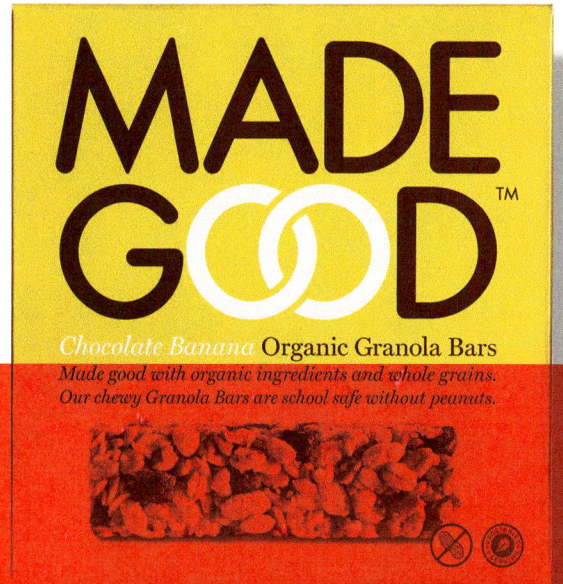

Chocolate Banana Organic Granola Bars
Made good with organic ingredients and whole grains.
Our chewy Granola Bars are school safe without peanuts.

Concrete
a creative brand agency.

concrete.ca

Index of people and places

Coal oven at Frank Pepe Pizzeria Napoletana, New Haven, Connecticut. Photo: Tom McGovern

Resources

Here is a list of some of the resources that were helpful in writing this book.

BOOKS

Bonci, Gabriele Pizza (Milan, 2012)

Buonassisi, Rosario Pizza: From Its Italian Roots to the Modern Table (Milan, 2000)

Helstosky, Carol Pizza: A Global History (London, 2008)

Masi, Paolo; Romano, Annalisa; Coccia, Enzo, The Neapolitan Pizza: A Scientific Guide About the Artisanal Process (Naples, 2015)

Pacifico, Francisco; Pacifico, Giovanni, Pianeta Pizza: La cultura della pizza (Naples, 2015)

WEBSITES

www.agrodolce.com (especially Gabriele Valdès' articles on pizza)

www.lacucinaitaliana.it (especially articles on Italian flatbreads by Massimo Lanari)

www.lucianopignataro.it

www.pizzanapoletanismo.com

www.SILVIOCICCHI.com

www.wikipedia.org

Massimo Bruno is a Toronto-based chef, event host and culinary tour guide. His focaccia barese enjoys legendary status with his fans we are honoured to reprint it here.

Michelle Capobianco is a chef, cooking instructor, culinary tour guide and owner of Majella Home Cooking. The images and recipe for torta al testo that appear in this book are reprinted from her companys' website.

Carmelita Cianci is an Abbruzzo-based editor and social media manager whose images of pizza scima abruzzese are reprinted from the website, Terre dei Trabocchi.

Viviana dal Pozzo is a Sicilian born, Verona-based writer/photographer whose crescia sfogliata urbinate (or crescia marhigiana) photos are reprinted from her terrific blog, Cosa ti Preparo per Cena?

Emiko Davies is a highly accomplished food journalist/photographer and author of two excellent cookbooks on Tuscan cuisine. Her article, pictures and recipe for focaccia di recco originally appeared on Food 52.

Bruno Di Sarno is a classically trained pizzaoiolo/chef/consultant here in Toronto. He's also an instructor at the School of Italian Pizza. Bruno (and Pizza School owners Francesco Zulian and Alice Rovere) provided valuable consultation during the writing of this book.

Gaia Massai is a Toronto-based wine and olive oil producer and importer and owner of Gaias Plate. Her delicious family recipe for cecina originally appeared on her company website.

Contributors

Ilaria Mazzoni lives in Emilia-Romagna. Her wonderful photos and description of piadina romagnola can be found on her blog, Ilaria's Perfect Recipes.

Chris Monette is a documentary and commercial filmmaker with over two decades' experience. Images and quotes from his Short Film About Pizza appear the Preface.

Sandra Panaggio's perfect image of schiacciata con l'uva fragola is reprinted from L'ho fatto io, a Giallo Zafferano blog.

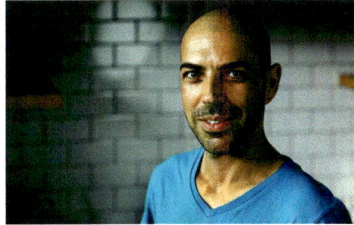

Luciano Schipano is a Toronto-based chef from Calabria, Italy, and owner of Schipano Fine Foods. His homemade pizza recipe and flour study (in the chapter on ingredients) are great additions to this book.

Sicily-based Sono Ylenia's photo crescentine modensi is reprinted from her blog, Dolcemente Salato.

Elvira Zilli is a food and lifestyle writer/photographer based in Rome, with a passion (and uncanny knack) for capturing poignant vignettes of the city's food culture. Her talents are on full display in the depictions of pinsa romana and pizza bianca that appear in this book.

THANK YOU

Thanks to the ICCO Board of Directors: Patrick Pelliccione, Tony Altomare, Joseph Balsamo, Giorgio Calorio, Daniela Carcasole, Alberta G. Cefis, Connie Clerici, Mary Dalimonte, Enrico De Pasquale, Antonio Di Domenico, John Fabbro, Greg Farano, Jenny Longo, Bambina Marcello, Mario Nigro, Corrado Paina, Ron Sedran, Richard Trevisan, Vittorio Turinetti Di Priero, Consul Giuseppe Pastorelli, Ambassador Claudio Taffuri.

Thanks to the staff of the Italian Chamber of Commerce of Ontario: Corrado Paina, Tiziana Tedesco, Giorgio Tinelli, Marisa Guida, Mary Chirico, Astrid Durzo, Marta Bertolo, Francesco Grimaldi, Marta Labate, Fereshteh Amiri, Marta Iannuzzi, Alberto Lanzi.

Thanks to the generous business, organizations and individuals that helped sponsor and contributed to the creation of Pizza Cultura: Mutti s.p.a., Le 5 Stagioni, Viva Napoli Pizzeria, Queen Margherita Pizza, Unico Inc.—Primo Foods, Antimo Caputo s.r.l., Pizza Nova, Nuova Service s.r.l., Aurora Importing And Distributing Ltd, Pizzeria Via Mercanti, Stelvio, Nodo Restaurant, Longo's, Cheese Boutique, Italiana FoodTech Inc / School Of Italian Pizza, Il Gatto Nero, Centennial College, Numage Trading Inc., Monte Carlo Inns, Sandra Pupatello, Italian Trade Commission, International Beer Brands Agency, King Street Food Company, Faema, Liberty Group, Massimo Bruno, Gaia Massai, Luciano Schipano, Rocco Agostino, Ettore Pugliese, Elena Di Maria, Melissa McCaughey, Bruno Di Sarno, Chris Monette, Luca Gatti, Quality Cheese, Vesuvio Pizzeria and Spaghetti House, Ciao Roma, Sud Forno, Terroni, Pizzeria Defina, Mattachioni, Superpoint, Descendant Pizza, Maker Pizza, Aida's Pine Valley Bakery, Grande Cheese, Double D's Chicago Style Pizza.

Acknowledgements

BOOK TEAM

BOOK CONCEPT
Corrado Paina, ICCO

WRITER
Mark Cirillo

PHOTOGRAPHER
Rick O'Brien

ADDITIONAL PHOTOGRAPHY
Victor Virgilio, Elvira Zilli,
Emanuela Storti, Emiko Davies,
Michelle Capobianco,
Viviana dal Pozzo, Ilaria Mazzoni,
Carmelita Cianci, Sandra Panaggio,
Sono Ylenia. Uncredited photos
are from Shutterstock.

The image on the bottom of page 107
is from "In Defence of St. Louis-Style
Pizza" Copyright © 2016 by Serious Eats.
Photo used by permission of the publisher.
Photo: Lopez-Alt, J. Kenji

FRONT COVER PHOTO Frank Pepe
Pizzeria Napoletana (archive photo)

BACK COVER PHOTO
Frank Pepe Pizzeria Napoletana
by Tom McGovern

ITALIAN INTERVIEWS
Translated by Mark Cirillo
and Marta Bertolo

PUBLISHER
Mansfield Press

EDITORS
Denis De Klerck, Anne Fullerton

COVER DESIGN
Concrete

BOOK DESIGN
Denis De Klerck

PROJECT COORDINATOR
Marta Bertolo

WEBSITE
Francesco Grimaldi, Valerio Baldissera

RICK O'BRIEN PHOTOGRAPHY

During his 20 years in the hospitality industry ranging from cook to restaurant manager, & everything in between, he comes by food photography honestly. With a couple of years cutting his teeth as the resident photographer at College Street's Orbit Room documenting live bands & industry characters, it was some career altering support from some of Toronto's finest architects that set him on the path he is today, documenting the design of revered restaurants/hotels/private-homes, capturing the plates & faces of star chefs, restauranteurs; traveling the world capturing lifestyle, personal/corporate portraits, & exclusive events. Rick & his team are always up for creating beautiful photography & film, no matter the subject, genre or place.

RICK O'BRIEN PHOTOGRAPHY

MARK CIRILLO

CUCINATO Mark is a Toronto-based writer and food industry consultant with a mixed bag of experience in publishing, marketing and content production. He's also the founder of *Cucinato*, a boutique agency that produces events, like olive oil and wine tastings, and various types of content, like articles and videos. Or a book like this one. It's all about connecting people with authentic experiences, helping them understand and appreciate artisanal foods, as well as the people who make them.

CUCINATO.CA